STRANGE BUT TRUE
LOUISIANA

SWEETWATER
PRESS

Strange But True Louisiana

Copyright © 2007 Cliff Road Books, Inc.

Produced by arrangement with Sweetwater Press

The TABASCO® marks, bottle, and label designs are registered trademarks and servicemarks exclusively of McIlhenny Company, Avery Island, LA 70513. www.TABASCO.com

ISBN-13: 978-1-58173-549-9
ISBN-10: 1-58173-549-9

Design by Miles G. Parsons
Map of Louisiana by Tim Rocks

Printed in The United States of America

STRANGE BUT TRUE
LOUISIANA

LYNNE L. HALL

SWEETWATER
PRESS

TABLE OF CONTENTS

Funny Happenings Here 125

ARKANSAS

LOUISIANA

MISSISSIPPI

TEXAS

In a Strange State:

Road Trip Through Strange But True Louisiana

Laissez Les Bon Temps Rouler!

OK. So, that's not the New Orleans tourism department slogan. Theirs is "Come Fall In Love With Louisiana All Over Again," an adequate slogan, we suppose. They've got slick ads and pretty television commercials—with lots of famous people telling you why you should come visit the state. They've got culture. They've got history. They've got natural wonders. Perfectly adequate, as we said.

Ah, but it misses something, no? We say it's just a tad ennuyeux for the state that taught an entire country how to party. Where's the music? Where's the reveling in the streets? Where's the…Hey! Throw me something, Mista!

Louisiana, and the Big Easy, in particular, took a big hit recently. But even as mean a party pooper as Katrina can't kill the spirit of the people who gave us Mardi Gras, "the greatest free show on Earth." It may have been scaled down, but only a few months after the devastation of the most active hurricane season in recorded history, the show did go on. Despite the doomsayers, who predicted the death of the city, a myriad of bureaucratic snafus, and the heartbreaking ruin, New Orleans is recovering. Forget those rumors that there's nothing left. Her heart is there, and soon she will reclaim her reputation as The City Care Forgot.

New Orleans isn't the only fun to be had, either. The whole state has an enormous joie de vivre. As you travel from place to place, the names sing-song a Zydeco melody to you: Acadia. Calcasieu. Breaux Bridge. Natchitoches. Tangipahoa. Ponchatoula. Cocodrie. Aiiieee! Then there's the food! Cajun or Creole, whatever you call it, ca c'est bon!

And, that's just the beginning. The tourism department won't tell you about it, but Louisiana is a state of pure wackiness. It's a state filled with eccentric characters; crazy happenings; extraordinary, weird, sometimes even spooky, places; and some of the most bizarre landmarks ever built.

So, forget those slick ads. Turn off the pretty television commercials. Come with us on a tour through Strange But True Louisiana. We'll let the good times roll!

Strange Statues

We've Got Statues

Scattered willy-nilly across Strange But True Louisiana is an eclectic collection of strange and quirky monuments.

LOUIS ARMSTRONG • NEW ORLEANS

Louis Armstrong was born in New Orleans in 1901. He grew up in poverty, learning to play the cornet during one of his many stints at the New Orleans Home for Colored Waifs, a place he was sent for general delinquency. He began playing the New Orleans clubs and saloons in his early teens and by the early 1920s, was touring the country, leading his own band.

Beginning as a trumpeter, he was an innovative performer, whose charismatic personality and musical

Louis Armstrong was the most famous jazz musician of the twentieth century.
Courtesy of Louisiana Office of Tourism.

skills are credited with transforming jazz from a tough regional dance music into a popular art form. He was the most famous jazz musician of the twentieth century.

His moniker "Satchmo" was a shortening of his childhood nickname "Satchelmouth," which was a comment on the size of his embouchure—that shape the mouth makes when playing a wind instrument. Armstrong's high-pressure approach to playing the trumpet damaged his embouchure to the point that, at times, he was unable to play, which led to an emphasis on his singing. His raspy voice gave the world some of its best loved music, including "Hello, Dolly," "When the Saints Go Marching In," and "What a Wonderful World." Those of us of a certain age remember him on numerous variety shows, trumpet in hand, white handkerchief wiping away sweat, and that gravelly voice delighting with his signature songs and quick wit. It's a piece of cultural history burned into a collective memory.

Armstrong died in 1971, but he's not forgotten in his hometown. New Orleans honors him with a statue and the Louis Armstrong Park. The bronze statue, just inside the park's entrance, depicts a dapperly dressed Armstrong holding a trumpet in one hand and his ever present handkerchief in the other.

Located on North Rampart Street.

BLIND JUSTICE • LAFAYETTE

We knew justice was blind, but we had no idea she was also empty-headed. In a step away from your usual statue of Lady Justice, artist Diana Moore sculpted two huge "architectural urns" for Lafayette's new courthouse. The sculptures, which flank the Federal Courthouse entrance, show Ms. Justice from the neck up. She's blindfolded, as usual, looking, perhaps, more like a bandit than an instrument of honesty. And there's something else. The top of her head is missing. Yep. It's just gone. Nothing there but an empty space big enough to plant a tree in.

Located at 800 Lafayette Street.

SCHOLASTIQUE PICOU BREAUX • BREAUX BRIDGE

According to town history, Scholastique Picou, an Acadian woman, was young when she married Firmin Breaux and had five kids right off the bat. Firmin, you see, was an older fella, a pioneer who'd come to the area in 1771 and bought up land. In 1799, he built a footbridge across Bayou Teche to make passage easier for friends and family. Breaux's Bridge became something of a landmark around those parts.

Scholastique was still a young woman—just thirty-two—when Firmin died. There she was, a widow with five mouths to feed and no income. Ah, but she did have land and a lot of gumption.

She drew up the Plan de la Ville Du Pont des Breaux, the plan for the Village of Breaux Bridge. Her plan had a diagram of streets and a detailed map of the area and included land for a school and a church. It also included the bridge named for her late husband—hence the name of her village.

On August 5, 1829, Ms. Breaux began selling lots and the town of Breaux Bridge was founded. She later married and had two more children. Guess there was plenty of money to feed everyone by then.

A life-sized bronze statue of Scholastique Picou Breaux graces the town's City Parc. A labor of love, the statue was erected by a group of townswomen to honor the town's founder and a woman of gumption. They chose sculptor Celia Guilbeau Soper to render Breaux's likeness. In learning about her subject, Soper was shocked to learn that, not only was she Scholastique's great-great granddaughter, but she also shared her July 25 birth date. Since no pictures or likenesses of Scholastique existed, Soper used her own daughter as a model for the sculpture, which depicts Scholastique surveying her town, worn boots perched on a log and plans in hand.

BRIGADIER GENERAL CLAIRE LEE CHENNAULT • BATON ROUGE

Wondering why Chinese folks would give Louisiana a statue of one of Louisiana's most famous native sons? Here's why.

See, Claire Lee Chennault volunteered for the Army during World War I, but earned his wings too late to see combat. So, he served in the Army Air Corps for the next eighteen years, retiring in 1937. He was then hired by China, who had been at war with the Japanese for two years, to train its fighter pilots. Well, the Chinese Air Force collapsed, but, not one to throw in the towel, Chennault formed the American Volunteer Group— popularly known as the Flying Tigers. The group fought the Japanese over China, Burma, and India before the U.S. ever entered World War II. When the country did finally join the

fray in 1941, Chennault returned to the U.S. Army Air Corps
and commanded the 14th Air Force.

The Chinese people were grateful to Chennault for his
efforts in preserving their freedom. In 1976, the Republic of
China presented the State of Louisiana with the statue to
express their gratitude.

Located at the USS *KIDD* Veterans Memorial Museum at
305 South River Road.

EVANGELINE • ST. MARTINVILLE

Longfellow wrote his epic poem "Evangeline, A Tale of
Acadie" in 1847 after hearing about the Great Expulsion of the
Acadians. He entwined the fictional love story of Gabriel and
Evangeline with the nonfiction account of the expulsion. It
outlines the seperation of the lovers, thier eventual reunion, and
thier deaths.

Gabriel and Evangeline and their story were reinvented
several times in poems and stories and eventually fiction blurred
into fact. The story believed to be the "true story" of
Evangeline and Gabriel is Felix Voorhies's 1907 revision of
Longfellow's poem, titled "Acadian Reminiscences: The True
Story of The Acadians." Voorhies renamed the two Emmeline
Labiche and Louis Arceneaux, both common surnames in
Louisiana, and stressed Louisiana, and St. Martinville, in
particular, as the setting for his tale.

As the supposed backdrop for the lovers' drama, St.
Martinville is a treasure trove of Evangeline attractions
including the Evangeline Oak and the Longfellow-Evangeline

Strange Statues

State Historic Site, which offers an opportunity to see how Louisiana's first Acadians lived, with a visit to an early Creole plantation home.

And then there's the Evangeline monument, which many believe is placed atop the burial site of Emmeline Labiche. So many believed this to be the true site, in fact, that in the 1930s, a group of concerned French Canadians tried to get the remains returned to Nova Scotia. An uprising from St. Martinville citizens, however, scotched the plan.

Many people think the Evangeline monument is on top of the burial site of Emmeline Labiche.
Courtesy of Louisiana Office of Tourism.

The Evangeline statue over the "tomb" was created with money donated by actress Delores Del Rio, who starred in a 1929 movie version of the story. Del Rio herself was the sculpture's model. Inaugurated in 1931 in a gala affair hosted by Del Rio, it was placed on a pedestal beside the St. Martin de Tours Catholic Church.

Located on Main Street.

Frostop Root Beer • They're Everywhere!

Looks like the Jolly Green Giant had a thirst attack in a trip across Louisiana. He's left a slew of giant Frostop Root Beer glasses strewn around the state. Frostop Root Beer got its start in 1926, when Mr. L.S. Harvey opened his first stand in Springfield, Ohio. The smooth, creamy concoction was such a hit that Harvey began opening stands across the nation. That is, until World War II put a damper on things, what with all those shortages.

After the war, Harvey, convinced he had the best root beer around, picked up where he left off and, aided by the drive-in craze, began opening stands again. By the 1950s, his stands—topped by the huge frosty mug of Frostop Root Beer—dotted the countryside. They became

Frostop Root Beer Mugs are in several cities throughout Louisiana.
Courtesy of Frostop® Root Beer.

a favorite hangout and, despite the proliferation of fast food joints, many of the stands are thriving. Louisiana is lousy with 'em. You'll find Frostops in Algiers, Baton Rouge, Houma, Jefferson, La Place, New Orleans, Raceland, and Thibodeaux.

Strange Statues

HADRIAN • NEW IBERIA

So, what's a seven-foot-tall, toga-wearing Spanish Roman emperor doing smack dab in the middle of Cajun country? It's quite simple, really. You see, New Iberia was settled in 1779 by a group of three hundred Spanish settlers. It's the only Louisiana town to be founded by Spaniards in the colonial period.

New Iberia's one-ton statue was sculpted in 130 AD—with the real live Hadrian posing. See! We told you it was ancient. It's the only full-length statue of the emperor in the country and well worth a looksee on historical interest alone!

Located at 301 East St. Peter Street.

HAYRIDE STARS • SHREVEPORT

Have we taken a step back in time? There's a bunch of dead singers standing in front of the Louisiana State Exhibit Museum! They're really, really big singers, too—not only in fame, but also in stature, oh, wait, we mean statue!

The huge bronze sculptures of Hank Williams Sr., Johnny Cash, Buck Owens, and Hank Snow are part of a plan to commemorate the vital role Louisiana played in this country's musical history. You see, Shreveport is home to the Municipal Auditorium, site of the historic radio broadcast, the *Louisiana Hayride*. Surpassed in popularity only by Nashville's *Grand Ole Opry*, the *Hayride* helped to launch the careers of many of the nation's greatest musical artists, including Elvis Presley. Throughout its heyday from 1948 until 1969, the show was broadcast throughout the country.

Acquirement of the four statues, sculpted by artist Bill Rains, is just the beginning of the Foundation of Music, Arts, and Entertainment of Shreveport's plan to honor the *Louisiana Hayride*. The group plans to move the statues to the front of the Municipal Auditorium and hopes to commission twenty-five more star statues in the envisioned *Street of Gold* exhibit.

The statues are currently located at 3015 Greenwood Road.

EQUESTRIAN STATUE OF ANDREW JACKSON • NEW ORLEANS

Clark Mills was an innovative sculptor, they say, and one of his most innovative works was the equestrian statue of Andrew Jackson that stands in what's now called Jackson Square.

Back in the 1700s, the area that's now the square was a military drill field. It was called Place d'Armes until 1848, when it was renamed for Andrew Jackson—hero of the famous Battle of New Orleans. The good folks of New Orleans wanted a way to honor Old Hickory, so they commissioned Mills to build a statue—an equestrian one, like those over in England and France.

So he built his big bronze statue of Andrew Jackson bravely astride a rearing horse. "Oh, my!" said experienced equestrian artists. "But you have two of the horse's legs in the air!" "Well, duh," said Mills. "Can't rear with only one leg off the ground!"

No one thought that an equestrian statue could support itself on its two back legs. Mills proved them all wrong, and, hence, went down in history as the first artist to sculpt a rearing equestrian statue. And Andrew Jackson was the first statue to sit astride the first rearing equestrian statue.

Located on St. Peter Street.

Strange Statues

HUEY LONG • BATON ROUGE

Oh, Lordy! You scared me! You might get a start, too, when you enter Louisiana's Old State Capitol Building in Baton Rouge and find yourself being greeted by former Governor Huey Long. The man's been dead nigh on to seventy years, but he's still pontificating within the halls of the Old Capitol. OK, so he's a bit stiff, but you would be, too, if you had joints of steel.

The life-sized animatronic statue of Huey Long is located in a room on the building's west side. He's standing behind a podium, with an old-timey radio within his line of sight. Your presence in the room breaks the circuit of a light beam and suddenly the radio and Long come alive. Long converses with the radio announcer, whom he calls "Radio Boy," on five different subjects in one-and-a-half-minute intervals. To hear all five subjects, you must "play," by circulating through the room, looking at the pictures and clippings on the wall. This keeps breaking those light beams

This statue of Huey Long stands in the English Garden of the New Louisiana State Capitol.
Courtesy of Louisiana Office of Tourism.

and bringing Bionic Huey and Radio Boy alive. The subjects are diverse—from LSU football to Long's politics and his assassination.

That's not the only statue of Long. Outside the New Louisiana State Capitol stands a memorial for the man who commissioned its construction. The statue, which depicts Long holding a model of his monument, can be found in the English Garden.

The Old Capitol Building is located at 100 North Boulevard. The New Capitol Building is located at North 3rd Street on State Capitol Drive.

MAID OF ORLEANS • NEW ORLEANS

Everyone knows the story of Joan of Arc, woman of visions who believed she was called to fight for the King of France. You know all that stuff—accused of witchcraft, burned at the stake—right? Well, it was Joan, probably the first woman to lead an army, that wrested control of Orleans from England and returned it to France. Hence, the Maid of Orleans moniker.

So, the people of France gave the folks of New Orleans a magnificent statue of Joan of Arc. Brandishing a banner, the maid sits astride a rearing steed. It's an exact replica of the statue in Place des Pyramids in Paris. The statue arrived in New Orleans in 1958. Unfortunately, the city didn't have the $35,000 needed to have the statue erected. So, Joan languished in storage until then-French President Charles DeGaulle visited the fair city. He enjoyed his stay and was charmed by the town and when he returned to France, he began a drive to raise the funds to have the statue erected.

Finally, in 1972, Joan and her steed came out of storage and were placed on a seventeen-foot pedestal on the Place de France at the end of Canal Street, where it stayed until development necessitated a new location.

She's now in a place of honor in the French Quarter, a place where she fits in quite well, considering she was gilded in 1985. She and her rearing horse glint brightly in the Louisiana sun,

The Maid of Orleans, Joan of Arc stands proudly in the French Quarter.
Photo by John Craven, 2003.

beckoning visitors into the jewel of New Orleans.

Located on the corner of St. Philip and Decatur streets.

MONUMENT TO THE IMMIGRANT • NEW ORLEANS

This sculpture honors Italian immigrants who came to this country at the turn of the century, many of whom entered through the Port of New Orleans. The monument commemorates their bravery and sacrifice in giving up all they knew for the promise of a better life.

Fashioned from white Carrara marble, the statue rests on a series of risers made of blue stone and white marble. It depicts a family of immigrants facing the French Quarter. Floating over their heads, and facing the harbor, is a female figure the artist describes as a muse, but that many other take to represent Lady Liberty. Artist Franco Allessandri, himself an Italian immigrant, imbued the faces of his immigrant family with the determination and courage they possessed starting a new life. The muse he describes as a symbol of hope, and the star she holds represents guidance to the explorer in his desire to discover a new place where he can achieve his dreams.

Located within Woldenberg Park at 1 Canal Street.

MOTHER RIVER • NEW ORLEANS

The Mississippi River gave birth to New Orleans and, winding her way around the city, she has ever given it life. It's fitting, then, that the city honor its mother with a thirty-foot statue that greets maritime visitors at the mouth of the Port of New Orleans.

Titled *Mother River*, the sculpture depicts a female form reaching skyward from her northern tributaries to her destiny— the warm waters of the Gulf of Mexico. Her tributaries are represented as children clutching at her feet and along the base riverboats, tugs, and other vessels appear in relief.

A dramatic mixture of human drama and nature's challenges, the *Mother River* has been likened to another Lady standing in a harbor further north.

Located at 1350 Port of New Orleans Place.

Strange Statues

MUFFLER MEN • BOSSIER CITY/METAIRIE

What is this obsession with muffler men? Maybe it's the square jaw. Maybe it's that he's just so darn tall. We don't know, but whatever it is, Louisiana has a couple of the big hunks to assuage your craving.

A Cowboy Muffler guy stands guard over Bossier City. Wearing a yellow shirt, blue jeans, a black Stetson, and holding his lasso, the big guy stands in front of a trailer dealership.

Metairie's Muffler Man is tall, dark, and suave. Actually, he looks just a tad sleazy, what with that Snidley Whiplash mustache and those thick eyebrows. He's been helping hawk auto insurance since 1974!

OCEAN SONG • NEW ORLEANS

This stainless steel sculpture is an integral part of New Orleans's Woldenberg Park and helps to carry the aquatic theme of the park, which is situated along the Mighty Mississippi. Created by native New Orleanan John Scott, the sculpture consists of eight narrow, three-sided pyramids. Each ten feet tall, the highly polished surfaces reflect viewers' images and give a feel of gentle ocean movement, meant to symbolize man's connection to the sea.

Located at 1 Canal Street.

OLD MAN RIVER • NEW ORLEANS

When they say this is a "stylized stone human figure," boy do they mean stylized. The eighteen-foot, seventeen-ton monument is another statue meant to represent the Mississippi

River. If it does, then the Mighty Mississippi is a mean looking character. The expression on his face is quite disturbing. Maybe that's 'cause he's naked. And, he's got no hands. Supposedly, the statue's rounded body forms represent the river's power and majesty.

Located in Woldenberg Park at 1 Canal Street.

OUR LADY OF PROMPT SUCCOR • NEW ORLEANS

Miracles seem to abound around this venerable statue of the Virgin Mary, perhaps the nation's oldest. To begin with, it was a miracle that brought it here. In the 1800s, the Ursuline Academy, a girl's school founded by French Ursuline nuns in 1727—now the nation's oldest girl's school—was in dire need of teachers. To request help, Mother Saint Andre Madier wrote to her cousin, Mother Saint Michel Gensoul, who ran a girl's boarding school in France.

It was a simple request, you'd think. However, because of the French Revolution, not only was the Church short of help in France, but the Pope also was a prisoner of Napoleon. It would truly be a miracle if Mother Saint Michel was granted permission to go to America.

Ask and ye shall receive. Having been told that only the Pope could grant permission, and knowing there was barely a chance that the Pope would even receive her letter of request, Mother St. Michael prayed to the Virgin Mary—aka, Our Lady of Prompt Succor—that her request be granted. Well, lo and behold, she did receive papal permission to take a contingent of teachers to New Orleans. Before leaving, she commissioned a

Strange Statues

statue of the Virgin Mary holding the Infant Jesus. The statue was blessed and was brought to New Orleans on December 31, 1810, where it was installed in a place of honor at the school.

A few years afterward another miracle was attributed to the statue—or more correctly, we suppose, to Our Lady of Prompt Succor. According to legend, on the eve of the Battle of New Orleans, many New Orleans women and children gathered in the chapel of the Ursuline Convent on Chartres Street, praying before the statue of Our Lady of Prompt Succor that the Americans would be victorious. That night Mother Superior made a vow in the name of the community that if the Americans were victorious, the community would celebrate a Mass of thanksgiving every year afterward. They did win, and, from that date forward a Mass of thanksgiving is sung on the anniversary of the battle.

The venerable statue of Our Lady of Prompt Succor holds a place of high honor in the National Shrine of Our Lady of Prompt Succor, located on the campus of the Ursuline Academy.

Located at 2701 State Street.

ELVIS PRESLEY • SHREVEPORT

This statue stands outside the Municipal Auditorium—on Elvis Presley Avenue—where, as a virtual unknown, he made his debut on the *Louisiana Hayride*. It was October 14, 1954, and Elvis sang his newly recorded song "That's Alright Mama." According to *Hayride* legend, the song didn't go over that well. Elvis seemed nervous and his performance was a bit flat. During intermission, it's said, he hunkered down with Sam Phillips of Sun Records, who advised the kid to loosen up and be himself.

Elvis did just that and on his next performance, he knocked their socks off. He hip-strutted through "That's Alright Mama," and gyrated right into "Blue Moon of Kentucky." The audience was rocking in the aisle and a star was born. Elvis signed a contract to appear on the *Louisiana Hayride* every Saturday night for a year—at $18 a performance.

The bronze statue in front of the Municipal Auditorium was dedicated in 2004—the fiftieth anniversary of that landmark performance.

Located at 705 Elvis Presley Avenue.

Strange Statues

During the seventeenth century, a group of one hundred French families established an area of North America known as Acadia—now Nova Scotia. Situated on the frontier between the French and British territories, they often found themselves amid the conflicts between the two powers and were passed from one side to the other repeatedly. They survived by keeping a strict neutrality. In refusing to take up arms against either side, they became known as the French neutrals.

Unfortunately, that strategy came to an end in 1713, when France ceded the land to Britain for the last time. In 1754, the British demanded the Acadians swear an oath of allegiance to the British monarch, an action that would require them to take up arms against their friends and families in the French settlements. When they refused, they were expelled in an action known as "The Great Expulsion," in which twelve thousand Acadians were forced to leave. Families were separated, their homes were burned, and their lands were confiscated.

Canada's loss was Louisiana's gain. A large number of Acadians settled here, bringing their traditions, their cuisine, and their joie de vivre. Their coming shaped Louisiana's history and culture, transforming it from your garden variety Southern state into something more vibrant. Their music, their flavor, and their language dance in the breezes and beat in the heart of every Cajun.

Natural and Manmade Wonders

Wackiness abounds on the byways of our Strange But True Louisiana. No sappy theme parks here. Instead there's a weird hodgepodge of natural and manmade wonders.

ATCHAFALAYA BASIN • SAINT MARTIN PARISH

The Atchafalaya Basin, formed by the convergence of the Atchafalaya River and the Gulf of Mexico, is a grand national treasure. The nation's largest swamp wilderness at 800,000 acres, it's filled to the gills with all God's creatures great and small. The National Audubon Society, in fact, calls the fish and wildlife

The Atchafalaya Basin is the nation's largest swamp wilderness.
Courtesy of Louisiana Office of Tourism.

values of the Atchafalaya Basin staggering, reporting a lushness

Natural and Manmade Wonders

three and one-half times that of the Florida Everglades. A birdwatcher's heaven, it's home to three hundred species of birds, including endangered species, such as the bald eagle and peregrine falcon.

On the furry and cute side, there are deer, bears, beavers, minks, fun-loving little otters, bandit-faced raccoons, and sly foxes. On the scaly and scary side, there are slithery snakes and toothsome gators. And on the yummy side, there are shrimp, crawfish, and crabs. Best of all, you can get up close and personal with all of it.

There's a plethora of outfits offering swamp tours through the Basin. Boatbound, you glide through the maze of bayous and channels draped with curtains of Spanish moss, listening as the sing-song voice of your Cajun guide hypnotizes you with his tale of the swamp. There's so much to see and do, you may even decide you want to stay. No problem! Stay in one of the swamp cabins, many of which float right on the swamp, where you can feed the alligators from the porch.

AVERY ISLAND • IBERIA PARISH

Avery Island is the salt of the Earth. Literally. The island, first known as Isle Petite Anse, is actually a salt dome, created by the upwelling of ancient salt deposits that exist beneath the Mississippi Delta Region. This solid rock deposit, possibly an ancient buried seabed, is thought to be deeper than Mt. Everest is high. Covering 2,200 acres, the island is 160 feet above sea level at its highest point and is about two and one half miles across. It's one of five such domes in Louisiana.

Fossils found on Avery Island show that the salt springs attracted prehistoric settlers to the island perhaps 12,000 years ago. Evidence left by Native Americans indicate that the salt production industry here dates back to 1000 AD. According to legend, these natives had "mysteriously" disappeared from the island by the 1600s. By the eighteenth century, much of south-central and western Louisiana was inhabited by the Attakapas. There may be a clue to the mystery in the meaning of "Attakapas." It means "man eater," y'all. Yep, allegedly these guys were a ferocious bunch who liked nothing better than to dine on their enemies.

McIlhenny Company manufactures about 750,000 bottles of TABASCO® Brand Pepper Sauce each day on Avery Island, Louisiana.
Courtesy of McIlhenny Company.

Taking their chances on being eaten, white settlers moved into the area and soon discovered the salty island. In 1862, during the Civil War, the Avery family discovered a deposit of extremely pure salt just a short depth below the island surface. Today, Avery Island is home to one of the world's largest salt mines, operated by the Cargill Corporation.

Natural and Manmade Wonders

But as important as salt is, that's not what Avery Island is most famous for. No, that would be pepper. Well, pepper sauce, actually. Ever heard of TABASCO®? It seems the McIlhenny family founded a company on the island in 1868. As the family lore goes, founder Edmund McIlhenny had been given a few extra hot pepper seeds by a traveler from Mexico or Central America. Edmund planted the seeds and as they flourished, he began experimenting with pepper sauce recipes. When he finally hit upon one he liked, he began making it.

He bottled it in cologne bottles with sprinklers added to the tops, an important consideration, since his sauce was so concentrated that it needed to be sprinkled rather than poured. The sauce found its way to New York City, where a grocery wholesaler introduced it to the country.

Edmund began to sell his sauce locally, and by the early 1870s, TABASCO® was being sold throughout the U.S. and even in England. He had the forethought to patent his recipe and the process he used for turning peppers into his fiery red sauce. Today, his descendants are still using that basic recipe and process at the Tabasco Factory, which is open for tours.

The Tabasco Factory isn't the only reason for visiting Avery Island. Thanks to Edward McIlhenny, second son of Edmund, the island is a lush subtropical paradise within a paradise. Mr. Ned, as he was affectionately known, loved rare plants, and he enhanced the island's natural landscape with dozens of varieties of azaleas, Japanese camellias, Egyptian papyrus, and other rare specimens.

In addition, in 1892 Mr. Ned established a protected

rookery on the island. Distressed over the wholesale slaughter of the snowy egret for their feathers, which were used for ladies' hats, Mr. Ned caught eight young egrets, raised them in captivity on the Island, and released them in the fall to migrate with other species across the Gulf of Mexico. His efforts are credited with helping to save the snowy egret from extinction. Every spring thousands of egrets and other migratory fowl return to the rookery—now called Bird City—and rest up for their trip across the Gulf.

When, in 1942, oil was discovered on the island, Mr. Ned protected his paradise by insisting that production crews leave the live oak trees and either bury their pipelines or paint them green to preserve the beauty of the wildlife refuge. Like the Tabasco Factory, Jungle Gardens and Bird City are open to the public.

Wondering where the name TABASCO® comes from? Well, it was inventor Edmond McIlhenny's second choice. He first wanted to call his sauce Petit Anse Sauce. But when family members balked at having the name of the island used for commercial gain, he reconsidered. He settled on TABASCO®, instead. It's a Central American word that many scholars say means "land where the soil is hot and humid," an apt description of Avery Island, we say.

Natural and Manmade Wonders

BAYOU PIERRE ALLIGATOR PARK • NATCHITOCHES

Bayou Pierre Alligator Park has hundreds of alligators and they all must be hungry, for seemingly at every turn, you get to watch brave souls stuffing meat into their gaping maws. Chomp! Chomp! As you meander through the park, you see gators of all sizes, from teeny weeny little babies to great big mamas with teeth the size of sabers. The park also has scores of snakes, frogs, lizards, skinks, cayman crocodiles, and turtles for you

At Bayou Pierre Alligator Park, visitors can feed the alligators.
Courtesy of Louisiana Office of Tourism.

to get a gander at. And, if cold-blooded creatures give you the heebie-jeebies, relax. There's also a cute little raccoon village where furry raccoons live and play. There're also little pygmy goats and other warm-blooded creatures to pet.

You're also treated to educational lectures and videos throughout your tour. Oh, but, here's the best part! After you've fed the gators, you can go eat them! Yep, at the Gator Bites snack shop, you can chow down on tasty fried pieces of gators we can only assume were out on the farm chowing down with their buddies just days before. Don't miss the gift shop, where you can pick up a stuffed gator to go.

Located at 380 Old Bayou Pierre Road.

CARILLON TOWER • MORGAN CITY

Wondering just what a carillon is? It's an instrument comprised of at least twenty-five chromatically tuned bronze bells that are played manually by pulling a lever on a device called a "clavier." Cast from pure bronze and tuned to one one-hundredth of a tone, carillon bells are usually suspended from a steel frame that's adapted to the tower or belfry in which the bells are to be installed. Each bell's clapper is connected to levers on the clavier and by striking the appropriate levers, the carilloneur (sacre bleu!) can ring any bell and play any tune.

Carillon Tower has sixty-one bronze bells.
Courtesy of Louisiana Office of Tourism.

How did little Morgan City come to have such a thing of aural beauty? The tower and the 9.5-acre park in which it sits were a gift to the town from Claire Brownell, a member of one of Louisiana's pioneer families. The 106-foot Carillon Tower stands in the center of the park, its steel and concrete contrasting with the softness of nature proliferating around it. With sixty-one bronze bells, all of which were cast in Holland, it's one of the world's largest carillons. The bells represent five full octaves, and range in weight from eighteen pounds all the way to 4,730 pounds.

Unfortunately, the park no longer has a carilloneur, so there have been no bell concerts for many years now. However, the bells chime four times an hour, lending beauty to an already beautiful setting. And, hey, just like the nature it so wonderfully showcases, it's free!

Located at 3359 State Route 70.

Louisiana is the only state in the country that has "parishes" instead of "counties."

CITIES OF THE DEAD • NEW ORLEANS

What could be more fitting for our trip through Strange But True Louisiana than a chilling tour of New Orleans's cemeteries! True cemetery tours aren't unique. People make trips to Arlington all the time, you know. But where else can you find the tombs of pirates and voodoo queens? No where, we bet. And here, you'll see most burials are done above ground in tombs, since a high water table makes traditional burials just about impossible. The first such cemetery to open was St. Louis Cemetery No. 1, which opened in 1789. The walls of the cemetery are made of vaults stacked on top of each other. They were economical, and all but the poorest could afford to be buried in this manner. The wealthy families who could build ornate tombs and crypts.

Voodoo Queen Marie Leveau is buried here and hers is one of the most visited graves in the country. You won't have any trouble recognizing it. It's the one with lots of Xs drawn on it. Seems that back in the seventies, tour guides passed along the legend that if you left a money offering and marked the tomb with an X, the Voodoo Queen would

New Orleans' cemeteries seem more like cities of the dead.
Courtesy of Louisiana Office of Tourism.

grant your wish. The only wishes being granted, however, were the tour guides' wish for wealth, for they would return later to gather up the offerings. Placing an X there today will get you something—a $1,000 fine!

By 1820, what with constant floods, hurricanes, and deathly illnesses, St. Louis Cemetery No. 1 was running out of space. A new cemetery was begun. Laid out in a square, with house-like mausoleums lining named and sign-marked streets, St. Louis Cemetery No. 2 was, indeed, a City of the Dead. As the years passed, the tombs and mausoleums here became more elaborate and ornate, with crosses and all manner of intricate carvings and monuments.

The Metairie Cemetery, located on Metairie Road in New Orleans, was opened in 1872. This cemetery has the largest collection of elaborate tombs and funeral statuary in the city, including a pseudo-Egyptian pyramid and a marble monument that's sixty feet tall. In addition, some of the country and state's most famous people are buried here. A walk through will take you past the burial sites of Civil War heroes, jazz great Al Hirt, actress Marguerite Clarke, famed Storyville madam Josie Arlington, and no less than five Louisiana governors.

There are more than forty-two cemeteries of interest in New Orleans. There are plenty of guided tours available to take you through these Cities of the Dead, a good idea, considering there's sometimes danger lurking among the tombs. No, not from ghosts, but from muggers intent on stealing your hard earned vacation cash. Should that happen, perhaps you can call on ol' Marie Leveau to put a hex on the thief. Hey, it couldn't hurt!

CREOLE NATURE TRAIL • SOUTHWEST LOUISIANA

Come explore the Outback! Louisiana's Outback, that is. The Creole Nature Trail, the Gulf South's first National Scenic Byway, is a 180-mile loop through the some of the wildest terrain Louisiana has to offer. Starting near the town of Sulphur, the byway loops through the marshlands and bayous of Cameron Parish, ending along the Gulf beaches and Lake Charles.

All along the way, you'll be agog at all there is to see and do. Within the loop, there are three national wildlife refuges, and the area is home to more than three thousand alligator nests, making it one of the largest alligator homes in the world. But gators aren't the only creatures living here. The trail has been named one of the Top 40 Birding Spots in North America, with good reason. There're more than 250 species of birds here. There're also sixteen different species of mammals, ten species of amphibians and reptiles,

The Creole Nature Trail offers views of many animal species, including alligators.
Courtesy of Louisiana Office of Tourism.

seven species of marine invertebrates, and eighteen species of fish. There's thirty-nine species of mosquitoes. Don't forget the bug repellent!

Directional and informational signs placed along the trail inform you of turnoffs and areas where you can explore the creatures up close and personal. And if just looking at them isn't enough action for you, there are plenty of activities available, including boating, fishing, hunting, crabbing, and nature photography.

And don't miss the visitor's centers, where you can learn all about the history of Louisiana and its wildlife. At "interpretive" centers in two of the refuges, you'll find a strange but true presentation, conducted by a robo-tronic old Cajun woman. As she paddles her canoe through a marsh, she tells the tale of Southwest Louisiana, its wildlife and its culture. To "enhance" the experience, there's a display of real stuffed, uh, "preserved" indigenous wildlife.

As you drive along, take the time to stop in at the towns and rural communities dotting the byway and get to know the Cajun lifestyle—the people, the food, the music, and the fun. Spend some time here, and you learn what it means to "pass a good time."

The Southwest Louisiana Convention & Visitors Bureau is located at 1205 North Lakeshore Drive, Lake Charles.

FRENCH QUARTER • NEW ORLEANS

If when you hear "French Quarter" you think, "Bourbon Street," you've really got a quite limited view. For sure, Bourbon Street is the most famous—and the liveliest—strip, but the French Quarter encompasses a seventy-eight-square-block area, thirteen blocks long and six blocks deep. It's a gumbo-pot neighborhood, and, though named the "French Quarter," it's heavily spiced with French, Spanish, Cajun, and Creole influences.

Also known as the Vieux Carre (voo ca-ray), which is French for Old Square, the French Quarter began as a French territory in 1718. This legacy survives today in such landmarks as the Ursuline Convent and the St. Louis Cathedral, and in street names such as Bourbon and Royal.

In 1762, however, King Louis XV signed the area over to his cousin Charles III of Spain, a rule that lasted forty years. The fire of 1794 destroyed much of the Quarter's French colonial architecture and it was rebuilt to Spanish tastes, with stricter fire codes, which required that all structures be physically adjacent and close to the curb to create a firewall. The old French peaked roofs were replaced with flat tiled ones and wooden

Street performers are common in the French Quarter.
Courtesy of Louisiana Office of Tourism.

sidings were replaced by fire resistant stucco, painted in the fashionable pastel hues of the day. Throughout the eighteenth and nineteenth centuries the colorful walls and roofs were decorated with elaborate wrought iron balconies and galleries. Since the 1920s, these buildings have been protected as

Natural and Manmade Wonders

historic landmarks, and, when renovated, must be done to match the historical architectural style.

In 1803, the signing of the Louisiana Purchase began a new era for New Orleans. American culture began filtering in and the "glorious victory" of the Battle of New Orleans sealed the city's loyalty to its new nation. A golden era of prosperity was experienced by the French Quarter, as cotton, sugar, and other commodities poured into her harbor.

The good times ended with the Civil War and the Quarter began an economic decline. But by the early 1900s, with the advent of jazz music, birthed in nearby Storyville, it began a new legacy, nurturing musical greats, such as Jelly Roll Morton, Louis Armstrong, and other jazz and ragtime musicians. The music, the quaint surroundings, and partytime attitude attracted other creative types, such as Truman Capote, Tennessee Williams, and William Faulkner.

This was the birth of Bourbon Street as Party Central. Dixieland jazz burst from the open doors of night clubs and strip joints, and people reveled in the street. Throughout the decades, the French Quarter's carefree attitude and merrymaking reputation grew, enhanced by that yearly bash, Mardi Gras.

If you're driving to New Orleans on Interstate-10, don't look for the French Quarter exit. You'll fly right on past. Folks around here call the Quarter the "Vieux Carre," so that's what you have to look for. Hint: It's Exit 235.

If the atmosphere on Bourbon Street is not to your liking, there are twenty other streets filled with quaint historic buildings and shops to explore. The French Quarter has more than two hundred restaurants, serving everything from downhome to fancy schmancy food. And, as for music, well, take your pick. There's more than one hundred live music clubs, playing all varieties of blues, rock, jazz, zydeco, folk, and funk.

To really get the most of your visit, it's a good idea to take one of the many guided tours that are available. Whether its historic architecture, haunted houses, or sex, scandal, and politics that interests you there's a tour that will tell you all about it.

GLOBAL WILDLIFE CENTER • FOLSOM

At Folsom's Global Wildlife Center, giraffes and zebras and camels and hippity hoppity roos run wild and free on nine hundred acres of Louisiana landscape. It's the country's largest wildlife preserve, home to more than three thousand exotic, endangered, and threatened animals from all over the world. And, unlike all those wild safaris, where you see the animals attacking the man and machine, here you can get up close and personal without fear. Purchase a souvenir cup of feed, and you can even have them eating out of your hand.

Hop on the Safari wagon for the one and one-half hour tour through the preserve and learn how these animals interact in their natural environment. In no time you'll have zebras and elands running alongside. Watch out for those giraffes, too. They can snag a cup from long distances with those twenty-inch tongues!

Natural and Manmade Wonders

The Global Wildlife Center's mission is to educate people about animals and the dangers they face from humans. By offering hands-on education, the center hopes to foster concern for wildlife and its preservation. It's a noble mission that should be embraced, making the Global Wildlife Center a worthy stop on your tour through Strange But True Louisiana.

The Global Wildlife Center is home to more than three thousand exotic, endangered, and threatened animals.
Courtesy of Global Wildlife Center.

Located at 26389 Highway 40.

La Branche Plantation Dependency House and Nordlicht's Grave • St. Rose

The Dependency House and adjacent slave quarters are all that're left of the grand La Branche Plantation, built in 1792. Back in those days, it was the custom for many families to move the teenage sons out of the house, where their rambunctiousness and other activities were out of sight and mind. So, in effect, the Dependency House was a swinging bachelor's pad.

It's an interesting enough tour, what with Zachary's Taylor's bathtub being there and all. But that's not why we're including it on our tour. No, what got our interest was the small plaque near the entrance to La Branche that marks the resting place of Nordlicht, reputed to be Adolph Hitler's favorite horse.

So how does a German horse end up in Louisiana? According to legend, the U.S. Army claimed Nordlicht as a spoil of war and brought him to the U.S. He was bought by New Orleanan Walter Mattingly, who brought him to La Branche Plantation in 1948, where he lived out his years in leisure. It's rumored that he sired many a Louisiana racehorse. He died in 1968.

Located on River Road.

LAKE PONTCHARTRAIN CAUSEWAY

Since the founding of New Orleans, Lake Pontchartrain posed an accessibility problem. Throughout the centuries, many plans were proposed to fix the problem, but it wasn't until the 1950s that technology finally came up with a solution. The development of pre-stressed concrete finally allowed engineers to build a bridge that spanned the lake from Metairie on the south to St. Tammany Parish on the north end—a distance of 23.9 miles.

Opened in 1956, the first span of the Lake Pontchartrain Causeway served three thousand vehicles per day. As traffic increased, a second, parallel span was opened and northbound and southbound traffic were separated. The spans are eighty-four feet apart and are supported by more than 9,500 hollow pilings, fifty-five inches in diameter. The spans are an average of fifteen feet high, with three main ship passages, where the elevation is twenty-five feet. There are also two marine passes of fifty feet for larger boats and a drawbridge at the north end for the largest boats.

The Lake Pontchartrain Causeway is the world's longest over-water highway bridge.
Courtesy of Louisiana Office of Tourism.

The Lake Pontchartrain Causeway is the world's longest over-water highway bridge. Today, it serves more than 30,000 vehicles per day.

LASER INTERFEROMETER GRAVITATIONAL-WAVE OBSERVATORY • LIVINGSTON

The purpose of the Laser Interferometer Gravitational-Wave Observatory (LIGO) is to search the heavens for the existence of gravitational waves—something predicted by Einstein. To look for gravitational waves, you look for ripples in the fabric of space-time. These ripples are caused by gravitational waves emitted from some space catastrophe—a supernova, maybe, or the collision of two black holes. The waves ripple through space toward Earth, bringing information of the cataclysmic event that caused them and other valuable info on gravity and space. Cool!

To detect these gravitational waves, scientists have designed an intricate device. Actually, it's all done with mirrors. With the Laser Interferometer the time it takes light to travel between suspended mirrors is measured with high precision, using controlled laser light.

Livingston's observatory is one of only two in the nation. It's a bit incongruous, this high-tech facility, manned by serious scientists, rising up from the backwoods swamps of Louisiana. And, although these ultra-tech scientists have yet to detect even a hint of a gravitational wave, they've adopted a true Louisiana attitude. "Laissez les bonnes ondes rouler!" is their battle cry. It means, Let the good waves roll!

These folks are conducting serious science here, but they will take time out to give tours. But only on Fridays. And only with at least twenty-four hours notice.

Located at 19100 LIGO Lane.

LOUISIANA SUPERDOME • NEW ORLEANS

John J. McKeithen was another Louisiana governor that knew how to get what he wanted. Back in 1967, he attended a baseball game in the Houston Astrodome. Looking around him at all the people, the excitement, and the tourist dollars, McKeithen told some friends, "I want one of these—only bigger."

Natural and Manmade Wonders

McKeithen was aided in his scheme by New Orleans businessman Dave Dixon, who'd envisioned a dome that could bring a professional football team to the area. The two lobbied and got legislature passed

The Superdome served as a shelter during Hurricane Katrina.
Courtesy of Louisiana Office of Tourism.

allowing the dome. Construction began in August of 1971 and was completed in November of 1975. Its new team, the New Orleans Saints, played their first game on September 28, 1975.

Looking remarkably like a spaceship from a 1950s B-movie, the Superdome rises seventy-three feet into the New Orleans skyline. It covers thirteen acres, and with a total floor area of 269,000 square feet, it's the world's largest fixed domed structure. There's seating for a maximum of 72,000 fans. And when that many don't show, the place still looks crowded, for each seat is a different color from the one next to it, giving the illusion of brightly-dressed fans occupying them.

Although the Superdome serves as a venue for many activities, from basketball to rock concerts to the 1988 Republican National Convention, it's best known for football.

Of course, the New Orleans Saints play there, but in addition, more professional football Super Bowls have been played there than at any other sports facility. The Superdome has hosted college football's Sugar Bowl since 1975.

During Hurricane Katrina, the Superdome was designated as a "shelter of last resort," where more than nine thousand residents and 550 National Guardsmen rode out the stormy night. The numbers swelled to twenty thousand when the levees broke and the city flooded. Although the Superdome sustained roof damage, the most damage resulted from the huge numbers of people. The lack of power and water led to rapid deterioration of sanitary conditions and much damage was done before the people could be moved out to other shelters.

Despite repair costs exceeding $185 million, the Superdome reopened on September 25, 2006, when the Saints beat the socks off the Atlanta Falcons. Take that, Katrina!

Located at 1500 Podyras Street.

MARDI GRAS WORLD • NEW ORLEANS

Step into Mardi Gras World, and you'll feel as if you've stumbled into an alternate reality. Everything is so big! The colors! They're so much brighter! And will you look? That's Cleopatra next to Scarlett O'Hara! Everywhere you turn, there're wonders to be seen. Celebrities and cowboys. Gods and goddesses. This is where Mardi Gras is born.

Mardi Gras World is the studio of the famous Kern family, float builders extraordinaire. Founded in 1947 by Blaine Kern, the company is the largest float-building company in the world.

Natural and Manmade Wonders

Kern began by painting a mural on a hospital wall to defray the costs of his mother's medical care. His artwork was admired by surgeon Dr. Henry LaRocca, then-captain of the Krewe of Alla, the biggest parading organization of that time. LaRocca commissioned Kern to build eleven floats for the 1946 parade.

His floats were a gigantic hit and soon other krewes were vying for his wares. He was sent to Europe to study Carnival traditions in Cologne, Frankfurt, Valencia, and other cities. And, when he returned, he turned New Orleans's Mardi Gras traditions upside down.

Back in those days, the parade was closed to all but

Mardi Gras World is the largest float-building company in the world.
Courtesy of New Orleans CVB.

the elite of New Orleans society. The krewes were exclusive to the rich, who had money, but not a lot of imagination. Their floats were…well, boring. Not Kern's. His were vivid, living things, dragons and storybook characters with heads that turned and eyes that rolled. But, though they enthusiastically embraced his work, the krewes refused him acceptance.

So Kern decided it was high time the exclusivity come to an end. Along with a group of young businessmen, he started Bacchus, a krewe of the people, by the people, and for the people. The upper crust tried to keep them out by convincing companies not to rent tractors to them to pull their floats, but Bacchus persevered, bringing their own vehicles.

And that, in fact, sparked an idea to build floats and buy tractors to rent to others for the parade, opening Mardi Gras to the world. When Kern first began building floats, there were only a dozen parading krewes in New Orleans. Today, there are fifty-seven and the New Orleans Mardi Gras is the Greatest Free Show on Earth.

In addition to producing Mardi Gras floats, Kern's company, which now includes his sons, also creates figures for theme parks—including Disney—and businesses, such as restaurants and casinos, around the world. And you can see all of these wonderful creatures in every stage of their manufacture.

Located at 233 Newton Street.

OAK TREES • LAFAYETTE/ST. MARTINVILLE/MANDEVILLE

Nothing symbolizes the South better than the shady canopy of a live oak tree. Think about it. What's the opening shot of most any movie or documentary set in the South? Right. A copse of massive oaks, branches draped in Spanish moss, their canopies casting the landscape in deep shadow.

Because they're long-lived specimens, those same trees that have starred in so many films may well have begun life before the first white settlers set foot here. They've stood silent witness to the birth of a nation, served as noted landmarks, and shaded generation after generation of Southern family picnics. And Louisiana has a plethora of historic oaks scattered throughout its countryside.

The Evangeline Oak is the most photographed tree in the country.
Courtesy of Louisiana Office of Tourism.

Cathedral Oak–Located on the grounds of St. Johns Cathedral in Lafayette, this giant live oak is thought to be the third largest oak in the country. More than 450 years old, it stands 125 feet high, with a canopy spread of 210 feet. Its circumference measures twenty-seven feet, and one branch that spreads in a southeasterly direction is estimated to weigh seventy-two tons.

Evangeline Oak–this is the most photographed tree in the country. It's located in Evangeline Park in St. Martinville.

Seven Sisters Oak–Located in the Lewisburg area of Mandeville, on the shore of Lake Pontchartrain, this truly massive oak is the country's largest certified oak. It has a girth of thirty-eight feet and spans more than 130 feet from branch to branch. Its unusual name comes from the fact that for many years, it was thought to be a collection of seven oaks. Closer inspection showed it to be one tree with seven distinct trunks. It's thought to be more than 1,200 years old.

OLD GOVERNOR'S MANSION • BATON ROUGE

You gotta love a guy like Huey Long. He was a guy that knew what he wanted, and he wouldn't let anything, certainly not anything as inconsequential as a shabby old governor's mansion, stand in his way.

The Old Governor's Mansion was built to resemble the White House. Courtesy of New Orleans CVB.

Elected governor of Louisiana in 1938, Long petitioned for new digs, the old governor's mansion not being up to his standards. The legislature denied his request, stating that "As long as there's a house standing, you can't build another." Sounded like a plan to Long.

He reportedly released a team of prisoners to come in and dismantle the entire governor's mansion—all in one night. And the next day, he once again petitioned the legislature, for now, indeed, there was no house standing.

Natural and Manmade Wonders

The legend doesn't end there. Newly-approved money in hand, he found an architect, handed him a twenty dollar bill, and, pointing to the image of the White House on the bill, told him that was what he wanted. And he got it—actually, a facsimile of the White House as Thomas Jefferson originally designed it—all the way down to the Oval Office. There were, of course, a few changes, Louisiana style. Instead of the stately interior colors favored by that other house in Washington, the new Louisiana Governor's Mansion was painted in bright, some might even say, gaudy, colors—bubble gum pink, mint green, sunshine yellow, peach, and lilac. Even the tile is painted!

Made of stucco Georgian construction, the mansion has two stories, a basement, and an attic. Thirty-foot columns span the two stories and support a fancy schmancy gable showing a design of the Louisiana State Seal—a pelican feeding her young. Not only is it the Old Governor's Mansion, but it also serves as an old governor's museum, with each governor of the twentieth century either having a room or a display case dedicated to him.

Located at 502 North Boulevard.

OLD STATE CAPITOL • BATON ROUGE

Approaching the Old State Capitol Building, you almost expect to hear the blare of trumpets and see King Arthur and the Knights of the Round Table trotting out on their trusty steeds. For, high atop a Baton Rouge bluff, overlooking the Mississippi River, stands the Medieval castle that once served as Louisiana's State Capitol.

Designed by architect James Dakin, the Old State Capitol is a prime example of the Gothic Revival style that became popular in the mid-1800s. It has twin octagonal towers, with pennants flying, stained glass windows, and crenelated gables. All that's missing is the drawbridge.

Not everyone was a fan of the Gothic design, it seems. Writer Mark Twain called the building "a little sham castle" and an "architectural falsehood" that would have never been built, if Sir Walter Scott had not "run the people wild, a couple of generations ago, with his Medieval romances." We're not sure just what Scott did to tick Twain off, but obviously there was some bad blood there, don't ya think?

The Old State Capitol is an example of the Gothic Revival architecture popular in the mid-1800s.
Courtesy of New Orleans CVB.

In 1862, New Orleans was captured by Union Admiral David Farragut, and the seat of state government left Baton Rouge. The once grand capitol building fell to disrepair, becoming known as "the old gray castle." It was used first as a prison and later as a garrison for African-American troops under the command of General Culver Grover. While being used as a garrison, the building caught fire twice, leaving it a gutted shell, abandoned by the Union troops.

Ah, but fortunes do change don't they? By 1882, the seat of government had returned to Baton Rouge and the old gray castle was rebuilt, renovated, and renewed. Inside, a grand new spiral staircase and a stained glass dome were added. Today, they remain the focal point of the interior. The building served as the State Capitol until 1932, when Huey Long took office as governor and decided it was time for a change.

Louisiana's State Capitol is the tallest capitol in the country. Courtesy of Louisiana Office of Tourism.

Today, the building houses a museum—the Old State Capitol Building Center for Political and Governmental History, which includes that exhibit we mentioned. You remember, the one with Bionic Huey. That's not the only interactive exhibit, either. The place is lousy with 'em, covering everything from voting rights to the story of Huey's more infamous brother, Earl.

Located at 100 North Boulevard.

Rip Van Winkle Gardens • New Iberia

From the name, you might just think this place is a snoozer. You'd be wrong. But with all the beauty surrounding you, you won't be bored either. You might, however, decide it's a good place to spend twenty years, just letting the rest of the world go by.

Rip Van Winkle Gardens is located on Jefferson Island, another of Louisiana's salt domes. Originally named "Orange Island," it was purchased in 1870 by famed actor Joseph Jefferson, who built a winter home and spent thirty-six years vacationing here. Although Jefferson performed numerous roles in theaters around the world, he was most famous for his portrayal of Rip Van Winkle from the adaptation of Washington Irving's story. He played the role more than 4,500 times in his career.

After his death in 1905, the property was purchased by the Bayless family. In the 1950s, J. Lyle Bayless Jr. began developing the property around the home as a garden, indulging his love for camellias. Making them the floral emphasis, he filled his garden with many varieties and colors and landscaped a series of interlocking gardens featuring a vivid combination of camellias, azaleas, crape myrtles, and other plants. Opening them to the public, he named the gardens "Rip Van Winkle Gardens," in tribute to Jefferson.

Planning to spend his retirement on the island, Bayless built a home on Lake Peigneur, adjoining the gardens. His plans took a skid, however, in 1980, just nine months after completion of his dream home. A drilling rig pierced a giant cavern, and suddenly the lake started draining. Drilling rigs, and other equipment began swirling around, like water circling a drain, and his home and sixty-five acres of gorgeous gardens just disappeared.

Fast forward to today. Rip Van Winkle Gardens has been restored and reopened to the public, with extended facilities, such as a conference center, a café, and a bed and breakfast. The Joseph Jefferson Mansion, too, is open for daily tours.

Located at 5505 Rip Van Winkle Road.

STATE CAPITOL BUILDING • BATON ROUGE

When Henry P. Long took the office of governor in 1932, he decided the state very much needed a new capitol building. The present one was old, built back in the 1800s. Besides, it was a gaudy thing—a cheesy replica of a Medieval castle. So what if it was the middle of the Great Depression? This was an absolute necessity.

A special session of the legislature was called to vote on an amendment to provide the funds for a new capitol building. The first vote fell four votes short. A roll-call vote began, and with Huey Long in the back "encouraging" members to vote for his new office, they did.

The new capitol building was completed in just fourteen months. At 450 feet high, with thirty-four floors, Louisiana's State Capitol Building is the tallest capitol in the country. It took twenty-five train cars to haul in the limestone used on the exterior and interior. Marbles came from Vermont and as far away as Italy. The total cost for the building was $5 million.

Conclude your tour with a trip up to the observation deck on the twenty-seventh floor. Overlooking Baton Rouge at a height of 350 feet, the deck gives a spectacular view.

Located at 900 North 3rd Street.

WORLD'S SMALLEST CHURCH • POINT PLEASANT

The church was built by Anthony Gullo in 1902. Seems Mr. Gullo had been quite ill, and not ready to meet his maker just yet, he made an appeal to the Virgin Mary, promising that, should she intervene on his behalf and allow him to recover, he would build a chapel in her honor. Well, Gullo lived to see another day and, true to his word, he built the Madonna Chapel.

We guess, Gullo figured, since he'd made no promises about size, a small church would fulfill

Claiming to be the world's smallest church, the structure measures nine feet by nine feet.
Courtesy of Louisiana Office of Tourism.

his promise. A really small church. Gullo's original chapel was just seven feet by seven feet with five chairs. It was once illustrated in *Ripley's Believe It or Not* as the World's Smallest

Church. We're not so sure it still holds that designation, however, for when the construction of a new levee required that it be moved, it somehow grew in its new spot. Now it's nine feet by nine feet.

Mass is celebrated in the chapel once a year, on August 15, the Catholic Feast of the Assumption. It's also open daily (well, there's a key in the mailbox) for those seeking a "little" solitude.

Located on River Road.

Louisiana is home to a Strange But True society. Its members are just a tad wooden. You see, membership in the Live Oak Society, founded in 1934, is open only to Quercus virginiana, the live oak tree. The society was the brain child of Dr. Edwin Stephens, the first president of the University of Southwest Louisiana, whose appreciation of the live oak was inspired by a Walt Whitman poem.

To become a member of the society, a tree must be at least one hundred years old, which means it has a girth of at least seventeen feet. The society, which started with fourteen Louisiana live oaks, now has a membership of 5,434 in fourteen states.

Strange Museums

There's a strong sense of history here, as evidenced by the large number of museums throughout the state. But you won't find works by Picasso or Monet gracing these walls. Nah. We're much more interesting than that.

ARK-LA-TEX ANTIQUE & CLASSIC VEHICLE MUSEUM • SHREVEPORT

It's two. Two. Two museums in one! And it's every big boy's dream. You girls will enjoy it, too, even if you're not car buffs.

The Ark-La-Tex Antique & Classic Vehicle Museum is located inside the George T. Bishop Building, which was established in 1921. The fully restored building once housed the area's oldest car dealerships, the Graham Truck Brothers and Dodge Brothers Car Companies. Today, the former showroom and assembly areas house a collection of more than forty antique and classic vehicles, including vintage automobiles and motorcycles. In addition, you'll find a large collection of period costumes, antique tools, and vintage toys.

Also housed within the museum is the Shreveport Firefighter's Museum, which includes a collection of antique fire apparatus and antique firefighting equipment and memorabilia.

Located at 601 Spring Street.

Strange Museums

CAPTAIN HENDERSON KID'S CABOOSE • BERNICE

Still just a kid at heart? Then visit this toy museum, which boasts a large collection of childhood memorabilia from the nineteenth and twentieth centuries. Miss that Barbie doll your stinky little brother decapitated way back when? You'll find one just like it here. How, about you, stinky little brother? Wish you had back that G.I. Joe your sister flushed in retaliation for the Barbie doll stunt? No problem.

This may be the best museum ever. First of all, it's located inside a real train caboose—a 1939 wooden car that's probably the last of its kind. Then when you step inside you find toys in child-height displays, but, unlike most museums, you'll find no "Do not touch signs." In fact, touching—no, playing—is encouraged.

You enter the museum from the north end of the caboose, where you'll find toys from the nineteenth and twentieth centuries divided into time periods. More recent examples can be found in the southern part of the caboose.

Located at 4th and Louisiana Streets.

DELTA MUSIC MUSEUM • FERRIDAY

As the birthplace of legendary rocker Jerry Lee Lewis, the little town of Ferriday shook up the music industry and helped bring the world a whole new rockin' sound. There's still a whole lotta shakin' going on in this town of 3,500, with the Delta Music Museum.

The museum honors hometown heroes and cousins Lewis, Jimmy Lee Swaggart, and Mickey Gilley, and celebrates musicians of the Delta, all the way from Memphis to Ferriday.

Stepping through its entrance, you take a step back to the days when the Killer set great balls of musical fire with his frantic piano antics. Photos and interactive exhibits create a nostalgic atmosphere, where you can sing along to all those old songs that bring back so many memories.

As Ferriday's most celebrated son, Lewis holds a prominent position in the museum. His grinning mug, topped by that shock of unruly hair, is plastered everywhere. But he's not the only star here. Focusing on the history, music, and culture of the Louisiana/Mississippi Delta region, the museum showcases a number of musicians. Included are exhibits on Conway Twitty, Aaron Neville, Pee Wee Whitaker, Clarence "Frogman" Henry, and Jimmie Davis, Louisiana's Singing Governor.

Located at 218 Louisiana Avenue.

ROBERT GENTRY MUSEUM • MANY

Robert Gentry was a collector. He collected…stuff. All kinds of stuff. And, that's just what his museum is—a collection of all kinds of stuff. You'll find cool totem poles standing next to tall wooden

The Robert Gentry Museum houses everything form totem poles to Marilyn Monroe memorabilia.
Courtesy of Robert Gentry Museum.

Strange Museums

Indians. Cowboy boots and prehistoric Native American artifacts are all jumbled in with Marilyn Monroe memorabilia, Civil War mementos, and personal items that once belonged to country and western entertainers. Whether it be the sublime or the absurd, Robert Gentry collected it and he wants you to see it.

Located at 867 San Antonio Avenue.

HOUSE OF BROEL HISTORIC MANSION AND DOLLHOUSE MUSEUM • NEW ORLEANS

If dolls and dollhouses take you back to your childhood and give you a warm and fuzzy feeling, then this is the place for you. The Dollhouse Museum is the personal collection of owner Bonnie Broel, who claims to be a real Polish countess. The collection includes fifteen museum-quality dollhouses and more than fifty vignettes and room boxes. The showcase among all these showcases is the twenty-eight room Russian palace, which is ten feet tall and twelve feet wide. Each house and room is populated by dolls dressed in elegant costumes befitting their surroundings.

As an added bonus, when you visit the Dollhouse Museum, you are also treated to a tour of the House of Broel Historic Mansion (or maybe it's the other way around). The original antebellum home was built in the 1850s by a wealthy New Orleans plantation owner. In 1884, it was bought by William Renaud, who renovated it in an amazing feat of engineering. He had the home lifted and a magnificent first floor was added. Featuring ornate chandeliers and black marble fireplaces, the home's new grand ballroom was the setting for many lavish parties and weddings.

Tours of the house include a looksee into the upstairs family residence, one of the only private living quarters in the area that's open to the public. On display here is the Countess's collection of fine antiques, including a desk made for the Duke of Dresden and a swath of Egyptian fabric more than two thousand years old.

Located at 2220 St. Charles Avenue.

INTERNATIONAL PETROLEUM MUSEUM AND EXPOSITION • MORGAN CITY

With gas prices often topping three bucks a gallon and the big oil companies posting record profits, it might be difficult to recall that petroleum first came into use as a cheap alternative to whale oil. Heck, those of us of a "certain age" remember it being a nickel a gallon!

A trip to the International Petroleum Museum and Exposition will tell the story of the petroleum industry, from its birth as a cheap commodity through its maturity into an absolute necessity whose cost can bring world economies to their knees. The museum is located on "Mr. Charlie," the first transportable oil rig.

Back in 1947, the oil industry had just discovered the Gulf of Mexico off the coast of Morgan City as a prime oil drilling site. Eager to strike black gold, the oil companies would use any means—old naval vessels, leaky, patched-together boats—to get their drilling equipment out to where the oil was. Once out there they pretty much worked as they did on land, building their derricks and drilling wells, working them until they were dry. Then, they'd dismantle it all, load it back on their old boats and sail off to the next site. Drill and repeat. It wasn't cheap, it took up a lot of time, and it was a heck of a lot of work. There had to be a better way.

There was. And it was a native Louisianan who came up with it. Alan J. LaBorde designed a plan to put the entire drilling operation on a barge that could be floated to any site. Once there, water would be pumped into the barge to sink it. On the bottom, it became a staple platform from which to drill. Once the well was dry, the water would be pumped from the barge, it would be re-floated, equipment still aboard, and moved to the next site.

LaBorde's boss at his company Kerr-McGee thought the project sounded good, but that it wasn't really practical. Bet he was kicking himself pretty soon. LaBorde left the company and found Murphy Oil, a small Arkansas company that sunk half a mil into the project and helped LaBorde come up with more investors. Finally, in 1952 LaBorde had built his barge with its transportable rig, named "Mr. Charlie," in honor of the owner of Murphy Oil.

Who was going to take a chance on it? Shell Oil proposed a deal. If the rig worked as designed, the company would use it to drill the new field they planned in East Bay. With a whole contingent of oil industry folks and a group of media types in tow, LaBorde deployed Mr. Charlie successfully. He drilled that oil field for Shell and for the next thirty years, drilled oil for every major oil company.

Mr. Charlie revolutionized the offshore drilling industry, which got its start off the shores of Morgan City, and led to the technology still being used around the world today. But Mr. Charlie was built to drill oil in forty feet or less of water. And, eventually, oil drilling left the shallow waters. Mr. Charlie was left high and dry.

In 1986, it was offered to the Smithsonian Institute, which declined for lack of space for the 220-foot by 135-foot rig. Seems it was the scrap heap for Mr. Charlie. But a group of men who'd worked on the rig stepped in, creating the non-profit International Petroleum Museum and Exposition. Today, Mr. Charlie not only serves as the museum, housing petroleum industry artifacts, but he also serves to train oil field workers.

Located in 111 First Street.

MARIE LAVEAU'S HOUSE OF VOODOO • NEW ORLEANS

Legends swirl around Marie Laveau like steam from a boiling cauldron, intertwining tendrils of fact and fantasy that conjure a mythological woman of many paradoxes. The daughter of a wealthy plantation owner and his Haitian-born slave, Laveau was born in 1794 as a free woman of color. She was a devout Catholic, who attended church daily, yet she christened herself the "Popess of Voodoo," and was acknowledged as New Orleans's first, and reputedly most powerful, Voodoo Queen. Many feared the wrath of her magical powers, while others saw a soft side in her ministrations to the sick.

Tales abound of the rituals held on Congo Street, with frenzied, rum-fueled dancing and Leveau presiding from her throne, her snake, Zombi, coiled around her body. Her powers became legend, and soon the elite of New Orleans Society were knocking on her door, asking for spells, love potions, and curses on their enemies. Recognizing a goldmine when

Marie Laveau's House of Voodoo is located on Bourbon Street.
Courtesy of Louisiana Office of Tourism.

she saw it, Leveau began charging for her services, making her Voodoo's first commercial queen. For a time, she was acknowledged as the most powerful woman in New Orleans. In retrospect most agree her powers came mostly from the knowledge she gleaned from intimate gossip shared by the highly placed clients she served in her capacity as a hairdresser.

Although Marie Leveau died more than a century ago, some believe she's still around, weaving her spells and casting hexes. Many claim to have seen her wandering through the French Quarter, which makes sense, considering the Marie Laveau's House of Voodoo is located on Bourbon Street.

This combination voodoo shop and museum is a wonderfully quirky treasure trove of weirdness. Wanna practice a little voodoo? This is the place for you. You'll find everything you need to cast a spell or two. Boss been picking on you? Get you one of those voodoo dolls and stick a few pins in it. May not hurt the boss, but it'll make you feel better! You'll find candles, roots, oils, beads, bones, charms, even blood. Make up your own gris-gris bag to bring success, money, luck, whatever your little heart desires.

Around every corner, is some sort of creepiness.

Located at 739 Bourbon Street.

LOUISIANA STATE MUSEUM • BATON ROUGE

Death masks and trumpets. Shrimp boats and submarines. Headstones and tuxedos. Giant crawfish and Mardi Gras beads. Holy moley! Could there be a more disparate

The Louisiana State Museum contains several Napoleon artifacts.
Courtesy of Louisiana Office of Tourism.

collection? We think not. But as different as they are, these items all have one thing in common: They tell the story of Louisiana's unique history and culture. And you can find them—and many more unique items—in the Louisiana State

Museum, a new 69,000-square-foot complex filled with state artifacts and oddities.

Death masks! OK, there's only one, but, wow! It's Napoleon's! You see, because of its French roots, Louisiana is inevitably tied to the emperor who sold the vast area of the Louisiana Purchase to the United States. According to legend, a group of Napoleon's former officers living in New Orleans hatched a scheme to rescue him from exile on St. Helena Island and bring him to New Orleans, where he would live out his days in the French Quarter in a home given to him by the mayor.

Unfortunately, before the rescue party—a ship manned by Louisiana pirates—could set sail, Napoleon died. As was the custom of the times, a death mask, a plaster mold of the deceased face, was cast by British surgeon Francis Burton, with Napoleon's personal physician, Francesco Antommarchi, in attendance. Later, Dr. Antommarchi made bronze and plaster copies of the original mask. In 1834, Dr. Antommarchi traveled to New Orleans, where he presented the city with a bronze copy of Napoleon's death mask.

The mask held a place of honor at the Cabildo until 1853. It disappeared during the Civil War, obviously packed away somewhere, for in 1866, a former city treasurer spotted it as it was being hauled to the dump in a junk wagon. He took the mask home and displayed it in his home. Eventually, the mask ended up in the Atlanta home of Captain William Greene Raoul, president of the Mexican National Railroad. Fortunately, Raoul read a news article about New Orleans's search for its missing piece of history. A man of integrity, he returned it to its home.

In addition to Napoleon's death mask, the State Museum contains several other Napoleon artifacts, including instruments Dr. Antommarchi reportedly used in the emperor's autopsy and an elaborately embroidered bee that adorned Napoleon's coronation mantle. There's also Louis Armstrong's trumpet, and bluesman Buddy Guy's guitar. There's a forty-five-foot shrimp trawler and a huge Confederate submarine that was found in Lake Pontchartrain. From food to music to industry to natural resources to culture, every inch of Louisiana's rich heritage is represented here. It's a big state. So, plan a day!

Located at 660 North 4th Street.

LOUISIANA STATE PENITENTIARY MUSEUM • ANGOLA

At the Louisiana State Penitentiary Museum, visitors can purchase CDs of inmates performing prison songs.
Courtesy of Louisiana State Penitentiary Museum.

It doesn't get stranger but truer than this! A prison museum. Oh, better, a museum of what used to be known as "the bloodiest prison in America!" The exhibits are deliciously ghoulish.

There's, of course, a cell, so you can get a smidgen of an idea what it's like to be a prisoner, and exhibits featuring the deplorable conditions Angola's inmates once faced. You won't want to miss the exhibit on great escapes. This one features some items prisoners used to escape, such as a fake head and hand donned by one prisoner and the huge compressor that was on the back of a truck. Two prisoners cut a hole in the tank and hid in it to escape.

The prisoner weapons display includes makeshift guns, hatchets, and a whole slew of mean looking knives. There's a collection of farm tools used by inmates and a moonshine still.

But, the most macabre exhibit by far is the display of execution devices. Imagine yourself strapped into "Old Sparky," Angola's old electric chair. Shocking! Or think about being strapped down on the table, waiting for a cocktail of lethal chemicals to enter your bloodstream. Yikes!

All that's pretty strange, no doubt. But you know what's the strangest part of this really weird museum? They have a gift shop! And they sell all manner of Angola memorabilia, including inmate crafts, CDs of inmates performing prison songs, and books about Angola's bloody days. Get your Angola T-shirt here—"Angola. A Gated Community." You can take home one of those cool striped shirts. Just be careful to keep the receipt, so they won't think you escaped!

Located on Highway 66.

MARDI GRAS MUSEUM OF IMPERIAL CALCASIEU • LAKE CHARLES

Yeah, we know. There are Mardi Gras museums all over the state. We chose this one because it boasts of the largest collection of Mardi Gras costumes on the Gulf Coast. Located at the Historic School of Arts and Humanities Center, the museum offers a year-round taste of Louisiana's biggest party.

The museum consists of several rooms devoted to the major events of the Mardi Gras season. See how the costumes are made in the room devoted to Preparation and Costume Construction. Learn about the Twelfth Night, the beginning of Mardi Gras. You'll also find a tribute to area Krewe Captains and a Walk of Fame, highlighting the history of all area krewes.

Located at 809 Kirby Street.

MEMORIAL HALL CONFEDERATE MUSEUM • NEW ORLEANS

The Memorial Hall Confederate Museum was opened in 1891 by Confederate veterans looking for a place to store all their Civil War stuff. It's now the oldest continually-operated museum in the state, with the second largest collection of Civil War memorabilia in the country.

One of the most revered of the exhibits is the display of Jefferson Davis items. Davis, President of the Confederacy, died in New Orleans in 1889. His body was interred at Metairie Cemetery for four years before being moved to Richmond, Virginia. Before his burial, Davis lay in state at Memorial Hall for more than a day, while sixty thousand people filed past to pay their respects.

The spot where his body laid is now a Jefferson Davis shrine, featuring items donated by Davis's wife, who, because of her love for New Orleans, sent her "dearest relics." Included in the display are evening clothes, a top hat and cane, a saddle, and, of all things, a crown of thorns given to

Strange Museums

Davis by Pope Pius IX. The display also features the Mardi Gras jewels and dress worn by daughter Winnie, known as the "daughter of the Confederacy" because she was born during the Civil War.

As much loved as was Davis, that's just how hated Union General Benjamin Butler, nicknamed "The Beast," was for his barbaric behavior during the Union occupation of New Orleans. During his reign in New Orleans, among other acts, he plundered and pillaged the city and its citizens, turning families into the streets to starve; wrongfully imprisoned innocents and sentenced them to hard labor; and hung Southern patriot William Mumford for the heinous act of tearing down the U.S. flag.

The Butler display in the Memorial Hall Confederate Museum includes such items as a segment of the U.S. flag torn down by Mumford, a set of silver spoons plundered by Butler, and a rare lithograph of "Fleurs du Sud," Flowers of the South. In this artwork, flowers are strategically placed in the likeness of the Confederate flag, an attempt by New Orleaneans to covertly display their patriotism.

The museum contains thousands of artifacts, from flags to clothing to rare weapons and photographs, with more than one thousand items on display at any given time. The displays are rotated and changed regularly, so even if you've been there, you haven't seen it all.

Located at 929 Camp Street.

MUSEE CONTI WAX MUSEUM • NEW ORLEANS

This isn't your usual wax museum. Don't come looking for sculptures of Michael Jackson or Princess Di. True, there are famous folks here, but only those famous folks who've figured into three hundred years of New Orleans history, beginning with local legends Iberville and Bienville discovering the swampy site of the soon-to-be-established city.

As you visit each succeeding vignette, the history of New Orleans unfolds before you. Here's the duc d'Orleans planning out the city. There's the casket girls, young women reportedly imported from France by the Ursuline Convent, to serve as suitable wives for the rowdy men of New Orleans.(The Ursuline sisters deny having any part in this). They were called "casket girls" because of the narrow wooden chests, called cassettes, that held the dowry from King of France the "filles de cassettes" supposedly brought with them. There's Napoleon signing the Louisiana Purchase! Jean Lafitte! Andrew Jackson in the Battle of New Orleans! Keep going and you'll find more modern players, such as Louis Armstrong and Pete Fountain and current heroes.

In a nod to the kids—big and small—who may find New Orleans history just a bit tame, you can follow up with a trip to the Haunted Dungeon, which features figures of famous horror characters of film and literature. Frankenstein, Dracula, and the whole gang is here.

The museum houses 154 life-sized sculptures, each made of bees wax mixed with a "secret" chemical compound that hardens it and raises its resistance to temperature changes. Its fleshy color is infused just beneath the last layer, giving it an uncannily realistic translucence. Each strand of the real human hair is inserted separately and all male statues have complete beards. Even those that are clean-shaven have a faint stubble. The eyes are all medical glass eyes imported from Germany, which is famous for its superior optical glass.

The museum offers special tours, the most popular of which may be the Voodoo Tour. Guests explore the rituals and revelry of Voodoo as they tour the museum's Legend Room. Sipping on special "love potions," they learn the history, rituals, and tales of New Orleans Voodoo. Following a tour of the museum, the spirit of Marie Laveau appears and entertains with a dance in front of her sculpture.

Located at 917 Rue Conti (Conti Street).

NATIONAL WORLD WAR II MUSEUM • NEW ORLEANS

Established to commemorate "The War That Changed the World," the National World War II Museum is the only museum in the country that honors all the amphibious invasions of World War II. Why the amphibious invasions? Because, according to General Dwight D. Eisenhower, the ability to land forces on far away beaches is what won the war. Why New Orleans? Because this is where Andrew Higgins designed and built the revolutionary LCVP (landing craft, vehicle, personnel) boat that made those beach invasions possible.

Higgins's design was based on boats used in swamps and marshes, with a major modification. Shown pictures of Japanese boats with ramps in the bow, Higgins designed his boat with a ramp that dropped down, so that troops and equipment could be deployed from the front instead of being laboriously lifted over the side. The prototype was tested on Lake Pontchartrain and 20,000 boats were built by Higgins Industries and its licensees.

In 1964, Eisenhower told Steven Ambrose, who was teaching in New Orleans, that "Andrew Higgins was the man who won the

D-Day is the central theme of the World War II museum.
Courtesy of National WWII Museum.

war for us. If Higgins had not designed those LCVPs, we would never have landed over an open beach. The whole strategy of the war would have been different." The statement is what inspired Ambrose to start the National World War II Museum. With D-Day as its central theme, the museum honors Higgins and pays tribute to American industry and the more than one million people who took part in the day that changed history.

Located at 945 Magazine Street.

NEW ORLEANS HISTORIC VOODOO MUSEUM • NEW ORLEANS

The New Orleans Voodoo Museum chronicles the historical importance of Voodoo in New Orleans. It's a dark and dusty place, filled with items of the occult from all over the globe, including, reportedly, some personal items of Marie Laveau.

Strange Museums

There's a Voodoo priestess on site most of the time, who will give you a reading or prepare a special gris-gris bag for you. And if you really, really wanna get scared, they can arrange for you to attend a real live Voodoo ritual!

Located at 724 Dumaine Street.

NEW ORLEANS PHARMACY MUSEUM • NEW ORLEANS

The New Orleans Pharmacy Museum was built in 1823 for Louis Dufilho Jr., the country's first licensed pharmacist. Although Dufilho studied medicine in Paris, from the collections of potions and remedies found in the museum, it's obvious he learned much from New Orleans's African population. He used the courtyard as a garden, where he grew plants and herbs he concocted into medicines.

Visitors of the New Orleans Pharmacy Museum journey back to the 1800s.
Courtesy of New Orleans Pharmacy Museum.

Dufilho, a French-trained pharmacist, and the many others that followed were responsible for the introduction of the soda fountain. Dufilho himself did not have one in his pharmacy. To help their remedies go down easier, they often mixed them with soda water spiked with flavoring. One of the most popular sodas contained a combination of cocaine, which was legal back in those days, and caffeine, a compound that was often prescribed for headaches.

Opened in 1950, the museum contains one of the largest pharmaceutical collections in the country. There are medical artifacts and an interesting exhibit on epidemics that plagued New Orleans. The building is filled with magnificent hand-carved rosewood cabinets made in the 1860s. These cabinets house hand-blown apothecary jars containing original ingredients used to make medicinal compounds. You get a shiver up your spine the moment you step in the door and spot the very attractive ceramic urn sitting next to the old-timey cash register. The urn is labeled "Leeches."

Inside these cabinets, you'll also find attractive cosmetic jars from the era. Back in those days it was the pharmacist that compounded all those creams and make ups. The ghoulish among you will be happy to find a large array of bloodletting devices and barbaric surgical and two-hundred-year-old dental instruments, including some used during the Civil War. There's also a display on the development of visual aids, including the Rosenthal Spectacle Collection.

Upstairs, you'll find a nineteenth-century "sick room," OBGYN exhibit, and other medical memorabilia. And, don't miss the walk through the courtyard, where the plants Dufilho once used as medicines are still being grown.

Located at 514 Chartres Street.

Strange Museums

OLD ARSENAL POWDER MAGAZINE • BATON ROUGE

Well, here's an explosive museum. It once held enough gun powder to blow up a good portion Baton Rouge, we bet.

Although the building known as the Old Arsenal Powder Magazine wasn't built until 1838, the site has a rich military history. Because its location on the banks of the Mississippi gave it strategic importance, each of Louisiana's ruling governments, from 1779 on, established a stronghold here. These governments include France, England, Spain, the brief reign of West Florida, the U.S., and the Confederacy.

The fourth building on the site, the Old Arsenal Powder Magazine was built by the U.S. Army engineering department. It is one of just two buildings surviving from the Baton Rouge arsenal and ordnance depot, which once garrisoned an infantry regiment, an artillery company, and six cavalry troops.

The list of military leaders serving here reads like a Who's Who of American History: Soldier and explorer Zebulon Pike, George Armstrong Custer, P.G.T. Beauregard, Robert E. Lee, James Longstreet, George McClellan, Nathan B. Forrest, and Zachary Taylor, who was living at the post when he was elected president of the United States.

The Old Arsenal building was almost lost to posterity when Huey Long, with grandiose plans for his new capitol, wanted to demolish it. He was dissuaded by Edward McIllhenny and other prominent Baton Rouge citizens. In 1956, the Daughters of the American Revolution took over its care, restored it, and established it as a museum, with displays on Baton Rouge's military history.

Located on Capitol Lake Drive.

W.H. Tupper General Merchandise Museum • Jennings

The W.H. Tupper General Merchandise Museum is housed inside an authentic country store that W.H. Tupper operated here from 1910 until 1949. The store, which operated through the Depression, sold everything— groceries, medicines, meat, hardware, dry goods, and clothing. Sound familiar?

When Tupper closed the store in 1949, the complete inventory remained on the shelves until 1971, when it was packed away and stored until Tupper's grandson donated it all for the opening of the museum. Touring the museum is like taking a step back to the early twentieth century. There are drugs and toiletries, such as Bayer Aspirin, twelve for three cents, and Ivory Soap, two bars for a nickel.

The collection of antique toys includes a kewpie doll, antique checkers, a wind-up Charlie McCarthy doll, and a wind-up Popeye and Olive Oyl toy. Olive Oyl plays the accordion while Popeye dances a jig.

In addition, the museum contains the Coushatta Tribe of Louisiana Basket Exhibit. The exhibit, on loan from the Tupper family, contains baskets made by the Coushatta Tribe that were sold in the store in the 1940s. There also are tribal artifacts, dance regalia, photographs, and Native American dolls on display. In all, the museum contains ten thousand original items, all of which were on sale at the time the store was closed.

Located at 311 North Main Street.

Strange Museums

Louisiana State University's Tiger Stadium, better known as "Death Valley," strikes fear in the hearts of college football fans everywhere.

Even in the South, where tailgate parties start as early as Wednesday before a Saturday game, LSU's fan enthusiasm is notorious. Not only is the noise level deafening, but those folks can make the Earth move. Literally. It happened on October 18, 1988, in a battle with Auburn University. When quarterback Tommy Hodson connected with a winning touchdown pass to Eddie Fuller, the LSU crowd erupted in an explosion so thunderous it caused an earth tremor that registered on a seismograph in the Department of Geology across campus.

Tiger Stadium was built in 1926, with a seating capacity of 12,000. As the sport's popularity grew in the South, so did the stadium. Recent additions—only briefly delayed by Hurricane Katrina—brought capacity to 91,644, making it the fourth largest stadium in the country. That's a lot of frenzied fans screaming, "Geaux, Tigers, Geaux!

The Haunting of Louisiana

Mist rising on moonlit nights. Ghostly apparitions floating through hallowed halls. Strange and scary noises. Louisiana can be a spooky place at night. With a past so rich in history, it's no wonder there are haints wandering this land. Here's just a smattering of Louisiana's legendary ghost tales.

ARNAUD'S RESTAURANT • NEW ORLEANS

Louisiana has a number of haunted restaurants. How encouraging! Nice to know there's fine dining in the afterlife. That's certainly the case with Arnaud's Restaurant. Established in 1918 by wine salesman Arnaud Cazenave, Arnaud's is synonymous with New Orleans haute cuisine. Count Arnaud, as he became known despite a lack of any true claim to the title, believed dining should be more than just an act to fill one's belly. It should an act of pure pleasure, an experience to be savored in leisure and a joy to all the senses. This was the experience he offered all his customers—superb cuisine served in grand French style.

Count Arnaud passed the restaurant to his daughter Germaine, who carried her father's legacy for many years. The Germaine Cazenave Wells Mardi Gras Museum was opened in her honor on the top floor of the restaurant. Open to the public during restaurant hours, the museum contains lavish Mardi Gras costumes owned by Germaine and her family.

When you put your heart and soul into something, no doubt a part of you lives on. And, so it is with Count Arnaud and Germaine. Many believe Count Arnaud is still around, ensuring that the food and service of Arnaud's remain up to his exacting standards. According to restaurant legend, many waiters over the years have been startled to see a

Arnaud's Restaurant is haunted by its former owner.
Courtesy of New Orleans CVB.

gentleman dressed in a turn of the century tuxedo standing at the beveled glass windows in the left corner of the dining room. He usually appears when the restaurant is especially busy and he's always wearing a big smile.

Happy, though he may be, he's not adverse to a little constructive criticism. If the setting of the napkins and silverware are not up to his standards, he has no qualms about moving them and he will rearrange the bar set-up to his liking on occasion.

Germaine, too, may be popping in and out. A misty figure has been seen several times wandering through the costumes in the Mardi Gras museum and on one occasion, a waiter saw a woman in a hat leave the ladies room, walk across the hallway, and disappear through the wall. Later investigation found that that particular wall was a recent addition and behind it was a staircase.

Located at 813 Bienville Street.

AVENUE INN BED AND BREAKFAST • NEW ORLEANS

This 1891 mansion is located on historic St. Charles Avenue. Its seventeen guest rooms are richly appointed with period pieces and contemporary accents. Sleep lightly if you stay there, for beds have been known to move on their own and singing has been heard coming from the old nanny's room. Pack that surge protector, for unexplained power surges are common.

At the Avenue Inn Bed and Breakfast, singing can be heard in the old nanny's room.
Courtesy of Avenue Inn Bed and Breakfast.

Located at 4125 St. Charles Avenue.

The Haunting of Louisiana

BRENNAN'S RESTAURANT • NEW ORLEANS

Brennan's is another legendary New Orleans restaurant. Opened in 1946 by Owen Brennan on a dare by Count Arnaud, it quickly became a French Quarter hot spot. Brennan's was heralded for its French cuisine created by Chef Paul Blange, whose favorite dishes included pompano en papillote, escargot, crepes, and flambes. A skilled and inventive culinary expert, he invented some of today's most popular dishes, including Bananas Foster and Eggs Hussarde.

After reading Francis Parkinson Keyes's *Dinner at Antoine's*, Brennan also came up with the idea of the gourmet breakfast. Breakfast at Brennan's, he called it. Not so original, but it was a hit, and word spread. Soon the elite of the elite were dining here, including Hollywood's brightest stars—Vivien Leigh, John Wayne, Barbara Stanwyck, Gary Cooper, and Jane Russell, just to drop a few names.

The restaurant was originally located on Bourbon Street, but when the lease was up in 1954, the landlord demanded 50 percent of the business, and Brennan decided it was time to move. He bought a building on Royal Street, a gamble, since the area was not a hot location, and began renovating. The new restaurant was scheduled to open in the spring of 1956. Unfortunately, Brennan was never to see the fruits of his labors. He died of a massive coronary in November 1955.

His family carried on, with sister, Ella, taking over management, and Brennan's Restaurant opened on schedule. Ella proved to be as able a restaurateur as her brother and under her management it continued its world-famous five-star status and was later taken over by Brennan's sons, who are the current owners.

Today, in addition to its legendary cuisine, Brennan's serves up a pretty good ghost story. According to legend, a couple of the restaurant's original employees have stuck around to make sure things are going as Owen Brennan planned.

Reportedly one of those employees is Chef Paul Blange. Legend has it that Blange was so devoted to the restaurant that when he died, a restaurant menu, a knife, and a fork were placed across his chest as he lay in his coffin. It's his spirit, folks say, that haunts the restaurant's kitchen. Many of the chef staff have reported the feeling of being watched and of a light touch as they are preparing meals. His shadowy figure has been seen here after hours, and he's been known to bang doors and pots in the empty kitchen.

Another former employee that seems to be still around is Herman Funk, a wine master who helped build Brennan's extensive wine inventory. He's still making choices, say employees, who dread going to the wine racks alone. Herman is there, clinking on the bottles to indicate which wine they should choose, and most say they take his suggestion, just to keep him happy.

For a really haunting dining experience, you might want to request the sumptuous upstairs red dining room. According to restaurant legend, this room was the site of a murder–suicide when the building was a private home. During the Civil War, the owner killed his wife and son and then hanged himself from the ornate brass chandelier. One waiter, a Brennan ten-year veteran, claims to have seen the man's ghost. It's so spooky the cleaning crew refuses to go there at night.

Located at 417 Royal Street.

BEAUREGARD KEYES HOUSE • NEW ORLEANS

Built in 1826 for wealthy auctioneer Jean LeCarpentier, this beautiful house gets its name from two of its more famous former residents. Confederate General P.G.T. Beauregard reportedly lived in the house from 1866 until 1868, while he was president of the New Orleans, Jackson, and Great Northern Railroad. Author Francis Parkinson Keyes used the home as a winter residence for more than twenty-five years during the early 1900s. She wrote several books here, including *Dinner at Antoine's* and *Blue Camellia*.

Now a beautiful museum, the Beauregard-Keyes House is reputed to be haunted—quite gorily haunted, as a matter of fact. The first haunting may have something to do with General Beauregard. According to legend, sometimes at night, the mansion comes alive with the sights and sounds of a bloody Civil War battle, though why this battle—complete with ghostly horses—is fought inside the house is anybody's guess. Wounded soldiers with blown away faces and mangled limbs shatter the stillness with their screams and the sounds of gunshot and cannon fire echo through the halls, all accompanied by the smell of blood and decay.

The home's grounds also are the site of a noisy battle, one of a more recent nature. Seems the garden was the site of a bloody mafia massacre, and the sounds of gunfire, along with the smell of gunpowder, and screams, can be heard emanating from here. At times, ghostly figures have been seen running madly through the gardens.

Located at 1113 Chartres Street.

1891 CASTLE INN • NEW ORLEANS

A mansion built during the Gilded Age, the 1891 Castle Inn is located in the exclusive Garden District. The owners say reports from guests of ghostly encounters prompted them to do a little research. As a result, they've learned the inn has two resident ghosts, both of which left the corporeal world more than one hundred years ago.

Reportedly, the first ghost is that of a carriage driver, who also served as a "gentleman's gentleman." He was a light skinned black man, who spoke several languages. And he loved the finer things in life—good music, aged whiskey, and lively women. He wasn't above playing a good joke every now and again, too. Unfortunately, it was his vices that did him in. Seems he got a bit inebriated one night and either fell asleep while smoking or turned over a heating pot—paranormal investigators found him a bit confused on the exact cause. Whatever it was that started the fire, he was too drunk to rouse himself and escape.

The owners find it only fitting that he haunts the main house, since he reportedly thought it his rightful place, instead of the servant's quarters. He's the one, they say, who is often heard whistling or coughing in the hallways. Many guests have reported seeing his form in mirrors and out of the corner of their eyes. And he still likes a good prank every now and again, fiddling with the radio, turning lights and ceiling fans off and on, and hiding stuff. In one reported prank, a guest hunted high and low for all the receipts from his and his wife's shopping to no avail, only to discover them hidden in the microwave.

The other ghost is that of a young girl who reportedly drowned in a small pond that graced the grounds of the original plantation. The pitter patter of her little bare feet can often be heard running up and down the hallways. She likes to jump on the beds, just as a live kid would, and startles female guests with light touches on their legs.

The owners stress that never have their guests had a frightening experience with their ghosts. Indeed it only adds a little spice to an already interesting stay.

Located at 1539 4th Street.

CHRETIEN POINT PLANTATION • SUNSET

Built in 1831 by Hypolyte Chretien and his wife, the feisty Felicite, the Chretien Point mansion served as a gorgeous centerpiece of a sprawling cotton plantation. Hypolyte may well have been a pirate at heart, for one of his best buds was the pirate Jean Lafitte, who visited often with his men. Felicite was a woman with a reputed fiery temper. The couple's arguments were loud and legendary.

By the time Hypolyte died of yellow fever, the plantation had more than five hundred slaves. Despite the fact that women were supposed to be shy and demure back then, Felicite took over management of the plantation without hesitation. She continued to entertain Jean Lafitte and his men, and she proved to be as good at cards as she was managing the plantation. She used her winnings to increase the fortune of her estate.

After the death of Jean Lafitte his men became a pack of renegades. Knowing of the fortune at Chretien Point, the band broke into the home one dark night. Expecting no resistance from a mere woman, they began to ransack the place. Hearing the commotion downstairs, Felicite grabbed a pistol and hurried to the head of the stairs. When the first pirate started up, she fired, taking off the top of his head. A trail of blood followed him in his tumble down the stairs. The other pirates fled.

The plantation passed next to Hypolyte and Felicite's son. During this time, a Civil War battle was fought on the grounds and the plantation was occupied by Union troops. A bullet hole remains in one of the front doors.

Today, Chretien Point Plantation is a popular bed and breakfast, owned by ancestors of Hypolyte and Felicite. The quintessential Southern plantation, it's well-appointed with period pieces. Its dramatic curving staircase served as inspiration for the sweeping staircase of Tara in the Hollywood movie *Gone With The Wind*.

It's that beautiful staircase that's the most haunted spot in the mansion. According to legend, the shooting incident is relived here often. There have been reports of the echo of a gunshot, followed by the thudding sound of the pirate's body hitting the ground. Additionally, it's reported that the bloodstains remain on the stairs, despite cleaning, and on the nights when guests hear the sounds of the terrible past events, those stains return to liquid.

Located a 665 Chretien Point Road.

THE CREOLE GARDENS GUESTHOUSE • NEW ORLEANS

This bed and breakfast is actually two historic 1849 mansions, coupled with a two-story servants' quarters. The two mansions couldn't be more different. The main manse was the home of Benjamin M. Palmer, a famous nineteenth-century minister. The rooms here are stately and elegant.

But the other, dubbed the Bordello Mansion, pays homage to New Orleans's storied red light district. Each room is named for and decorated in the style of a famous Storyville Madam.

The Creole Gardens Guesthouse is haunted by a servant woman.
Courtesy of Creole Gardens Guest House Bed and Breakfast.

Regardless of where you stay here, there's the possibility of a ghostly encounter. Numerous guests have reported sighting a servant woman dressed in gray with a white kerchief around her head. One guest even reported that this woman sat on the edge of the bed one night stroking her sleeping husband's face with a look of adoration, as if he were her sleeping child. Others have reported objects being thrown across rooms by unseen hands and the feeling of someone getting into bed with them.

Located at 1415 Prytania Street.

GARDETTE-LAPRETE HOUSE • NEW ORLEANS

Built in 1836 by a wealthy Creole named Jean Baptiste LaPrete, this luxurious mansion, Laprete's vacation home, was the center of Creole culture in the New Orleans of the 1800s. Unfortunately, Laprete's fortunes waned in the latter part of the century, and he found it necessary to rent out the home. But, he didn't rent it out to just anyone—only royalty was good enough.

Seems he rented the place to a mysterious Turk who claimed to be a deposed Sultan. The Sultan brought with him a fortune in gold and jewels, and he set about turning the home into his pleasure palace, complete with a harem and a bevy of eunuchs to guard the lovelies. He had all the windows and doors covered with heavy iron gates and men patrolled the grounds with curved daggers in their belts.

All those precautions came to naught, however. One bright morning a neighbor on her morning constitutional noticed a stream of blood running from beneath the iron gates of the home's grounds. When police arrived, they entered and found the gruesome scene of massacre. Blood covered the walls and floors and bodies were found strewn throughout the mansion. Each and every one had been hacked to pieces—all except the Sultan. He was found in a shallow grave in the backyard. Reportedly, he had been buried alive.

Although no one ever learned the reason behind the massacre, it was learned that the Sultan had a really big secret. He wasn't really a Sultan. That would be his brother. The brother whose gold and jewels he stole before skipping the country and coming to settle in New Orleans, probably thinking he'd never be found. There was speculation that the real Sultan had found his brother and exacted revenge. Regardless of whether it was the Sultan or a particularly violent group of robbers, authorities found that all gold, jewels, and other valuables were missing.

Throughout the years since the horrible carnage of that night, there have been reports of ghostly appearances of a strange man. He often has appeared at the foot of the beds of women living in the house. Sometimes bloodcurdling screams have been heard as well as the sound of Oriental music and the scent of incense.

Located at 1240 Burgundy Street.

Griffon House • New Orleans

The Griffon House was built in 1852 by Adam Griffon, who abandoned it just a few years later, fleeing the advancing Union troops. The house was confiscated by General Benjamin Butler, who turned it into a barracks for soldiers and prisoners.

According to legend, at this time there were a couple of soldiers in town who began looting some of the grand homes that had been abandoned by their owners. What the two didn't know was that Butler had passed a decree that anyone caught looting would be shot. Those good ol' boys did, indeed, get caught and were taken to the Griffon House. Throughout their incarceration, they repeatedly sang "John Brown's Body," a popular Yankee song.

The two were convicted of looting and were sentenced to be shot. Resigned to their fate, they bribed a couple of soldiers for two pistols and a bottle of whiskey. After drinking the whiskey, they lay on cots facing each other and simultaneously shot each other in the head. It was said the blood from their wounds poured down to the floor below.

But that wasn't the last heard from them. There have been ghostly happenings in the building since that grisly deed. One such happening occurred in 1936, when the house was being used as a lamp factory. A maintenance worker, alone in the factory, was working on the second floor. Suddenly the door of the room slammed open and he heard the sound of marching boots ascending the stairs. They stomped right into the room, followed soon by another set of boots coming up the stairs and into the room. Next he heard the sound of drunken laughing and someone faintly singing "John Brown's Body." The worker ran screaming from the factory and no promise of increased wages would convince him to return.

Another shrieking escapade occurred a few years later, when the house had been turned into a boarding home. A nice little lady had rented a downstairs room and had settled in quite contently until one night when she was sitting sewing by the window. She noticed a drop of blood on her arm. Thinking she must have pricked herself with the needle, she wiped it away, only to have it replaced by another. Then another. And another.

The Haunting of Louisiana

Yep, you guessed it. She looked up to find a pool of blood dripping down from the ceiling.

During the 1970s, the house was abandoned and its area became a haven for drug addicts. But soon, according to stories, even the addicts avoided the house because of sightings of two ghostly fellows in uniforms who walked through walls while singing some silly song.

The house was later bought and renovated by a local sculptor who denies any unusual happenings.

Located at 1447 Constance Street.

MYRTLES PLANTATION • ST. FRANCISVILLE

One of America's Most Haunted. That's the reputation of the Myrtles Plantation, a splendid bed and breakfast that's been featured in such prestigious publications as *Gourmet*, *Forbes*, and *Travel and Leisure* and on television networks, such as the A&E Network, the History Channel, and National Geographic. It was also a top feature in *The Haunting of Louisiana*.

It will be no surprise, then, that the resident ghosts have been seen, felt, heard, and smelled by guests, employees, and owners alike. The most famous spirit at the Myrtles is Chloe. Her story has been broadcast numerous times by the national media. She's thought to be a slave girl who worked in the home for the second generation of owners, Clarke Woodruff and Sara Matilda, daughter of Dave Bradford, who built the home in 1794. As legend has it, Chloe was briefly Clarke's mistress. When he tired of her and moved on to the next slave girl, Chloe was frightened that she would be sent back to the fields to work. She took to eavesdropping on Clarke and his family, in an effort to ascertain her fate. When Clarke discovered her listening one day, he cut off her left ear and sent her to work in the kitchen. From then on, she wore a green turban to hide the disfigurement.

There're different opinions on Chloe's motivation for her next act. Some say it was for revenge on Clarke. Others say it was a plan to worm her way back into the affections of the family that went awry. Whatever her reasons, it seems that Chloe picked some oleander leaves, which are poisonous, and baked

Myrtles Plantation is home to several spirits.
Courtesy of Louisiana Office of Tourism.

them into a cake. Perhaps she thought that the family would get ill and by nursing them back to health she would become a hero. She fed the poisoned cake to Sara Matilda and her two young daughters. All three fell ill and died the next day.

When the other slaves heard of Chloe's actions, they feared retaliation and hanged her from a tree, then weighted her body with rocks and threw it in the Mississippi River.

The Haunting of Louisiana

Today, Chloe, still wearing her green turban, is frequently sighted wandering the hallways and grounds of the Myrtles. She is often glimpsed in photographs. In addition, the Woodruff children are heard laughing and playing on the veranda, most often on rainy nights.

These aren't the only ghosts inhabiting the plantation. According to legend, a Civil War soldier who loved to smoke cigars, stayed at the Myrtles for a time. He died of battle wounds just outside the front door. Today, guests often get a strong whiff of cigar in his old room, despite the fact that the Myrtles is a non-smoking facility.

In 1871, then-owner William Winter was climbing the home's interior stairway when a mysterious assassin shot him through a window. He fell dead on the seventeenth stair. Reportedly, it's his footsteps guests hear climbing the stairs. The footsteps are reported to stop on the seventeenth stair.

In 1927, the caretaker was killed during a robbery. The owners say he's been seen at the plantation gates, telling people to leave.

The Myrtles Plantation has been a spirited place for quite some time, evident in several features of the house. Reportedly former owners had stained glass from a church installed because they believed it would keep ghosts out. In the nineteenth century, it was a common belief that spirits entered a home through keyholes. The keyholes of all the doors have a small cover over them. In addition, it was believed that ghosts hid in the corners of homes until nighttime, when they would come out to scare occupants. As a result, custom plasterwork, with special nun and cherub charms, was installed to keep ghosts out of corners.

All that effort and nothing works, for the spirits of the Myrtles Plantation seem to come and go at will. No doubt, the present owners are rather happy about that, though. Their ghosts are a pretty good marketing tool.

Located at 7747 U.S. Highway 61.

OAK ALLEY PLANTATION • VACHERIE

Oak Alley Plantation is named for the avenue of oak trees leading up to the palatial home. The trees were planted in the early 1700s by the first settler to own the land. The plantation home was built in 1832 by Jacques Telesphore Roman and wife Celina, who insisted on only the best. The result was the envy of all their friends. Celina dubbed her home Bon Sejour, French for "pleasant journey."

Jacques died of tuberculosis in 1848, sparing himself the trauma of the Civil War.

Visitors at Oak Alley Plantation once saw a candle thrown across the room by an unseen hand.
Courtesy of Oak Alley Plantation.

The Haunting of Louisiana

Celina and son, Henri, weathered the war at Oak Alley, but were forced to sell in the turmoil of Reconstruction. The plantation passed through several hands before being bought in 1925 by Mr. and Mrs. Andrew Stewart, who restored it to its former glory. Today, operated by a non-profit organization, the home is a living-history museum, open daily for tours.

Oak Alley has a reputation for being a very haunted house, though no one is sure just whose spirits are doing the haunting. Throughout the years, there have been reports of the image of a woman dressed in antebellum clothing looking from windows, the sound of invisible horses and carriages approaching the mansion, the sighting of a ghostly man dressed in gray sitting in the kitchen, and the sound of crying. On one particularly haunting occasion, thirty-five people taking a tour of the mansion watched as a candle was thrown across the room by an unseen hand.

Located at 3645 Highway 18.

Eat, Drink, and Be Merry!

Jambalaya. Gumbo. Oysters Rockefeller. Muffuletta. Po'Boy. Red beans and rice. Bananas Foster. Beignet. Louisiana put the spice in American cuisine. Here's a sampling of the state's restaurants and bars. Some are historic. Some are haunted. And some are just plain fun.

ACME OYSTER HOUSE • NEW ORLEANS

It doesn't look like much on the outside. And it's not much better when you finally make it inside. But once you bite into one of the ACME's specialty dishes, you'll be glad you waited in the always-present line. If you're a purist, down a dozen raw. Nothing better than these slimy little bottom feeders, dunked in cocktail sauce so

ACME Oyster House is worth the wait.
Courtesy of ACME Oyster House.

horseradishy it makes your eyes water, and downed with a pitcher of beer.

Or maybe you'd like a little Cajun Sushi—Oysters on the half shell (or fried if you're really squeamish) or shrimp—served with wasabi, TABASCO®, soy sauce, and chop sticks.

Then there's the huge variety of Po' Boys—a Louisiana submarine. You'll find everything, from fried oysters to soft shell crabs to ham or roast beef. If you're trying to watch your girlish figure, you can even get that with marinated grilled shrimp or chicken.

The French Quarter's oldest oyster bar, the ACME has been spiffed up a bit since Katrina, but it's not much changed. It's still loud and lively, with good ol' oysters and beer.

Located at 724 Iberville Street, 3000 Veterans Blvd, and 1202 N. Hwy 190

According to some accounts, it was Louisiana bad boys who gave the world one of its tastiest treats. Seems that after a night out drinking with the guys, these boys would bring home an oyster loaf as a "pour boire," a peace offering.

Another account has the term "po' boy" being coined in a New Orleans restaurant owned by a former streetcar conductor. In 1929, during a four-month strike against the streetcar company, the former conductor served his old mates free sandwiches. His workers referred to the strikers as poor boys and soon the sandwiches took on the name.

ANTIONE'S •
NEW ORLEANS

Talk about historic! Antoine's is the country's oldest family-run restaurant. Established in 1840 when New Orleans was queen of the Mississippi, it began as a

Antoine's is the country's oldest family-run restaurant.
Courtesy of New Orleans CVB.

pension, boarding house, and restaurant opened by New York native Antoine Alciatore. Soon the delectable aromas emanating from Antoine's kitchen established Pension Alciatore in New Orleans cuisine.

The restaurant became so popular that it quickly outgrew its location, moving just down the street, and then again in 1868 to its present location on St. Louis Street. When Antoine, knowing he was dying, left for France in 1874, he turned the restaurant over to his wife, who passed it on to their sons, who passed it on to theirs, and so on.

Antoine's has thrived for more than 160 years. The restaurant has witnessed the great moments of history—the Civil War, Prohibition, the Great Depression, two World Wars, the creation of Oysters Rockefeller. Oh? You're unfamiliar with that moment in history? Well, let us enlighten you.

It was 1899 and Jules, Antoine's son, was head chef at Antoine's. Escargot was a popular dish, but escargots were in short supply and Antoine's needed a substitute. Jules, an inventive fellow, came up with a new dish using oysters. Since his new dish was quite rich, he named it Oysters Rockefeller, after the country's richest man. Knock-off versions of the dish, many of which contain spinach to get the signature green color, are served all over the world. But Antoine's insists they are just pretenders. The original—which does not contain spinach—is a closely held family secret.

Today, Antoine's is synonymous with fine dining. Food is only one element, however. Seated in sumptuous elegance, surrounded by photographs of kings and presidents and stars, you can't help but hear the muted whispers of those who've come before you. The food, the elegance, the history. They combine to create a magical experience.

Located at 713 St. Louis Street.

CAFÉ DU MONDE • NEW ORLEANS

Forget Starbucks. The Café Du Monde is the original coffee stand. Immortalized in song (by Jimmy Buffett) and literature, it first opened in 1862 next to the French Market on the banks of the Mississippi. Locals and visitors stopped in here for a cup of strong French roast coffee cut with chicory, first added for economics—to stretch expensive coffee beans—but kept for the flavor it added.

Almost 150 years later, they're still stopping in. Although the Café Du Monde has recently added a few iced coffees to their fare, their signature drink is still Café Au Lait. It's chicory coffee stronger than any gourmet espresso drink, cut half and half with hot milk. That's usually ordered with a weird doughnut

Enjoy café au lait and beignets at Café Du Monde.
Courtesy of New Orleans CVB.

called a beignet—square, no hole, covered with a snowy mound of powdered sugar, served hot. It's a little bit of heaven on Earth.

Yes we know the Café Du Monde has opened several new stores, but you wanna go to the original at the French Market. It's located at 800 Decatur Street.

CENTRAL GROCERY • NEW ORLEANS

Another treat Louisiana has given the world is the muffuletta, a huge round sandwich. The sandwich was invented in 1906 at the Central Grocery, a small neighborhood grocery owned by Sicilian immigrant Salvatore Lupo.

Eat, Drink, and Be Merry!

Described as "one of the great sandwiches of the world," the muffuletta is made on a muffuletta, a type of Sicilian bread that's a large, round, flat loaf, spilt horizontally. There are variations today, but Lupo's original was—and still is—covered with layers of four types of meat and topped with provolone cheese. The whole thing is smothered in Central Grocery's signature olive salad, a mixture of olives, celery, cauliflower, carrots, olive oil, and seasonings.

You'll find that Central Grocery has changed little since making its contribution to gastronomic heaven. It's still a grocery—where you can pick up a jar of their olive salad—and they still make the best muffuletta in town. They have added some seating—a few mismatches stools pulled up to a counter—but your best bet is to get your Muff to go. (Unless you're really hungry, order a half. They're really big sandwiches!) Stroll over to Jackson Square and enjoy a taste of New Orleans. Just don't forget to pick up plenty of napkins. All that olive oil can make for a messy meal.

Located at 923 Decatur Street.

CHECKPOINT CHARLIE'S • NEW ORLEANS

Been putting off doing your laundry because it's just so boring? Have we got the place for you! Bring along those unmentionables and listen to some really rad alternative music while your clothes do the rinse-and-spin in the backroom laundromat.

Don't let the dark, biker bar appearance of the place intimidate you. It's a fun spot that's popular with the locals, especially the college crowd. There's good music, good food—burgers and such—and pool tables and video games. And, it's open twenty-four hours. So, it matters not what time of the day you run out of clean underwear. Just gather up a few loads and come party while you wash.

Located at 501 Esplanade Avenue.

CLOVER GRILL • NEW ORLEANS

Tired of all that fancy schmancy health food that's good for your heart but hard on your wallet? Then come to the Clover Grill, where the motto is "We love to fry and it shows." Even better, you can get a good giggle while you clog your arteries.

Opened in 1939, the Clover Grill is a twenty-four hour diner. It's small, just eleven stools against a counter and four tables. But the loud and boisterous staff makes you feel instantly welcome. Bogieing to your table to the high-powered dance music on the juke box, your waiter dispenses the laugh-a-minute menu. Along with the diner's fare, you'll find a few admonitions: "If you're not served in five minutes, it may be another five. Relax. This isn't New York." "Dancing in the aisle only. Please keep off the tables." "Please keep hands on top of the table. No talking to yourself." "We don't eat in your bed. Please don't sleep at our table." It's even better than the Bourbon Street show passing by the window.

True to their motto, you'll find typical diner comfort food. Breakfast is served any time and you can get your eggs with a pork chop or battered chicken fried steak. There's also build-your-own omelets and waffles that you can get plain or with ice cream, fruit, or nuts added.

Eat, Drink, and Be Merry!

The Clover lays claim to the "World's Most Delicious Burgers," and who are we to argue? You can get the house specialty, a mushroom cheeseburger, or build your own, with such additions as jalapeños, egg, or chili. What the heck, add it all! Throw in an order of sizzling hot fries and wash it all down with a good ol' chocolate malt. It's as the menu says, "Eat Well, Feel Swell." We'll worry 'bout those arteries later.

Located at 900 Bourbon Street.

COOP'S PLACE • NEW ORLEANS

When you walk into Coop's, you'll be expecting your typical bar fare. It's just a funky little hole in the wall, a little dark, with tables close together. Oh, but you're in for a surprise! Forget that typical bar food, Coop's kitchen is world-class.

Sure, you could get a burger, a good one, but why would you want to when there's so much more to be had? Coop's menu reads like one of those upscale "fine-dining" restaurants—except for the prices. Among the appetizers you'll find such offerings as smoked duck quesadillas, served with sour cream and Coop's own salsa or lamb ribs, served with red pepper jelly.

Coop's jambalaya is considered by many as the best in New Orleans. It's made in the Cajun tradition with boneless rabbit and smoked sausage, filled with celery, onions, peppers, and chopped green onion.

The Redfish Meuniere is an eight-ounce filet, floured and sautéed with a tangy shrimp and butter sauce. And then there's Coop's twist on an old Southern favorite. The Cajun fried chicken is seasoned with a secret blend of spices and served with rabbit and sausage jambalaya. There's shrimp Creole, beef tenderloin, pork chops, fried oysters, and a good supply of sumptuous pasta dishes—and an impressive wine list to accompany it all.

Coop's Place is a favorite with the locals. After your meal, you can join them at the bar or play a little pool or video poker and drink beer and sing to the jukebox. It's an all around fun French Quarter hangout.

Located at 1109 Decatur Street.

COOTER BROWN'S TAVERN AND OYSTER BAR • NEW ORLEANS

Ever wished you could belly up to the bar with the Duke? Maybe share a suds with Peter Sellers or kick back with ol' Tricky Dick? At Cooter Brown's you can have a beer with your favorite dead celebrity—or below him or her to be exact.

Every place needs a gimmick, and Cooter Brown's is dead drinking celebrities. The caricatures with big heads and small bodies are made of clay and acrylic paint. Holding a beer that connects somehow, they're hanging all over the walls of this zany tavern. It's fun to make the rounds, trying to figure out just why they're drinking that particular beer.

If you're a beer connoisseur, you'll love Cooter Brown's, dead celebrities or no. The place features 400 brews, with 350 of them imported and 43 on draft. It's also a pretty fun place to party, having been voted by *Gambit* magazine as New Orleans's number one place to get a cold beer, the number one sports bar, the second best place to shoot pool, and the third best place to get raw oysters.

Located at 509 South Carrollton Avenue.

CRAWFISH TOWN USA • BREAUX BRIDGE

The folks at Crawfish Town will tell you they serve the biggest crawfish in the world. No doubt about it, heaped up on a platter, all red and steaming fresh from the boiling pot, they do look almost big enough to pass for their close cousin, the lobster. Get 'em cooked any ol' way you like 'em, from baby-mild to Oh, Mama! hot.

In addition to boiling their bugs, Crawfish Town serves 'em up in a variety of Cajun cooking, including jambalaya, etouffee, boudin, and gumbo. You can get 'em boiled. You can get 'em fried. You can get 'em in a stew. You can get 'em in a pie. You can even get 'em made into a really tasty burger!

If crawfish isn't your thing, don't despair! There's plenty else to choose, from rib eyes to pork tenderloin, soft shell crab, and shrimp, and if you're really not adventurous, you'll even find grilled chicken. For dessert, I'd try the baked bread pudding. It's smothered in rum sauce.

Located at 2815 Grand Point Highway.

D.I.'s CAJUN RESTAURANT • BASILE

It all started way back in 1970. Disco music was in. So were miniskirts and platform shoes. Daniel Isaac (D.I. to all who knew him) Fruge was a young man, just getting started in his life as a farmer. He raised soybeans and rice and, in a forty-acre pond, he raised crawfish, harvesting them by tossing them into a small boat he pushed ahead.

To help out with the bills, D.I. set up tables in his farm equipment building on Saturdays and had himself a big ol' crawfish boil, selling those little suckers for the bargain price of five dollars for all you could eat. Word got out about D.I.'s special boil that seasoned the crawfish just right, and before long there were more people than his barn could hold.

In 1986, D.I. and wife, Sherry, decided it was time to make it official and opened D.I.'s Cajun Restaurant. Offering good Cajun food and a fun atmosphere, the restaurant was an immediate success, so much so, that two expansions were necessary in the ensuing years.

More than thirty years have slipped by, and we've seen some major changes in the world. But, there are some things that never change. D.I. and Sherry are still serving up some of the best Cajun food around. Crawfish and barbecued crabs and steak smothered in crawfish etoufee are just a few samples. They've added a stage to the restaurant that features live music most nights, with a Cajun jam night on Wednesdays. There's a big dance floor, too. So, when all the music reaches your feet, there's room for you to really move.

Located at 6561 Evangeline Highway.

DIVE INN GUEST HOUSE • NEW ORLEANS

Well, here's a place you can pack light for. Leave those swim suits (and the kiddies) at home, folks, because the Dive Inn is a place to forget your inhibitions and dive headfirst into your forbidden fantasies. Clothing is optional here. It may even be frowned upon. And PDAs (public displays of affection) are encouraged.

Once the home of the Mexican Counsel, the building has an old-New Orleans feel. You can walk out the door and cross the street to Pascal's Manale, one of New Orleans's finest restaurants. The ceramic tiled swimming pool was built in 1927. Its huge domed structure is an engineering marvel that was ahead of its time in technology. The charming rooms run the range from luxury to "poor man's" suite

Don't come here expecting your typical hotel-room stay. There're no TVs or telephones in the rooms. The owners, in fact, liken a stay here to commune living. The setting is intimate, relaxed, and stress-free (unless, of course, nudity stresses you out). And, you never know who your fellow guests might be. Musician Eric Burdon has stayed here. So has actor Dennis Quaid. So, pull out the small suitcase and get packing. Sybaritic pleasures await!

Located at 4417 Dryades Street.

HERBY-K'S • SHREVEPORT

Some may say it has a downhome atmosphere. Others may say it's a dive. But all say you gotta try the Shrimp Busters sandwich. It's the stuff culinary dreams are made of: jumbo shrimp, battered and fried light, stacked on buttery French bread, and smothered in red sauce. With onion rings and a frosty shake. You'll be dreaming of your next visit by the time you walk out the door.

Located at 1833 Pierre Avenue.

K-PAUL'S LOUISIANA KITCHEN • NEW ORLEANS

While Strange But True is the main criterion for inclusion on our tour, we'd be remiss if we didn't give a mention to K-Paul's Louisiana Kitchen. Its owner, Chef Paul Prudhomme was front and center in the 1980s, when the Cajun revolution brought Cajun cuisine to the world. His culinary masterpiece, blackened redfish, became a national craze so popular that it depleted Louisiana's supplies of the fish. Wearing his signature white beret and looking remarkably like rotund comedian Dom Deluise, Prudhomme soon gained

K-Paul's is famous for its blackened redfish.
Courtesy of Louisiana Office of Tourism.

international fame, appearing on popular television shows and in magazines.

K-Paul's (named for Prudhomme and wife, K) opened as a sixty-two-seat casual dining restaurant, and it wasn't long before the lines began to form. Back in the day, before expansion and reservations, diners often had to wait hours for a table—and wait they did.

Eat, Drink, and Be Merry!

Today, the 1834 building has been renovated and expanded to seat two hundred hungry diners and reservations are necessary. Although Prudhomme makes occasional appearances, the day-to-day operations are handled by Chef Paul Miller, who hails from Prudhomme's hometown of Opelousas.

Forget that casual dining thing. This is upscale Cajun cuisine, in a gorgeous setting. Don't come in wearing your Bermudas and flops, either. The attire is "business casual." It's worth the trouble, though, to find yourself seated on the lovely balcony, sipping wine, and tucking into some of the best food in the world.

Located at 416 Chartres Street.

LAFITTE'S BLACKSMITH SHOP • NEW ORLEANS

Legend has it that this mid-1700s building on the corner of Bourbon and St. Phillips Streets was operated as a blacksmith shop by Jean Lafitte's brother as a front for their privateering business. It's the oldest building in the French Quarter and is one of the few remaining original French-architecture structures, the others having been destroyed by one or the other of two devastating fires.

Now a bar and restaurant, Lafitte's Blacksmith Shop is a favorite haunt of locals, who like to begin and end their bar hopping here. Located at the far end of Bourbon Street, it's a bit of a stagger but worth the effort. As you step inside, you may well feel as if you've stepped back two hundred years. The interior is dark, lit only by candles. We guess that Lafitte's reputation as the most romantic bar in New Orleans stems from this flickering candlelight. Not only is it romantic, but it also hides a multitude of sins, giving the place another of its reputations—as a place where the locals lose their inhibitions.

If it weren't for the fact that you can feel a bit of dank cool air circulating, you might just believe the place hadn't been touched since Lafitte's brother hammered horseshoes at the centrally-located fireplace. Music plays on the juke box, and you can find an intimate table for a little drinking and spooning. Or stumble your way to the back, where there's a smoky piano bar and a

Lafitte's is known as the most romantic bar in New Orleans.
Courtesy of Louisiana Office of Tourism.

group of friendly folks ready to make you welcome. Sit at the piano and make your request. Better yet, join in with your own rendition. You won't be the only one there making a fool of yourself.

Located at 941 Bourbon Street.

NAPOLEON HOUSE • NEW ORLEANS

Remember how we told you about the scheme to bring Napoleon to New Orleans? And how the mayor was going to give him a house to live in? Well, this is that house! Of course, Napoleon never made it here, but so what? It was still going to be his house!

Napoleon House was built in 1797, with that generous mayor, Nicholas Girod, as its first occupant. Owned since 1914 by the Impastato family, it has become one of the country's most famous bars. With classical music—particularly "Eroiqua," which Beethoven wrote for Napoleon—playing in the background, the bar offers a dark and easy ambiance that draws a bohemian and eclectic clientele. It's been the hangout of writers, poets, and artists for decades.

The Napoleon House serves jambalaya, salads, gumbo, and sandwiches.
Courtesy of Napoleon's House Restaurant.

The Napoleon House Café serves jambalaya, salads, gumbo, and sandwiches, including a muffuletta that's said to rival that of the Central Grocery. Because of Katrina damage, the café and bar were operating on limited hours and Girod's Bistro, which offers fine dining, was temporarily closed at the time of publication. So check before you go.

Located at 500 Chartres Street.

NICK'S ON 2ND • EUNICE

Nick's Bar first opened in 1937 as a getaway for guys—no ladies allowed. Once a two-story building, it was a place where local men would gather to play Bouree and do a little male bonding.

During Prohibition, the upstairs was a speakeasy, where demon rum and other liquors were sold. Downstairs everything was nice and legal—just us guys playing a little cards, officer. If the revenuers showed up, a buzzer was pushed downstairs and all illegal activities ceased upstairs. No sir, Mr. Ness. Nothing going on up here. Nothing at all!

Today, Nick's operates in the original building, which was brought to Eunice on a horse-draw wagon, and true to its speakeasy roots, it's still a place to drink and have a good time. And you can get a darn good Cajun meal here, too, including crawfish etoufee and eggplant pirogue, a dish of battered and fried eggplant, stuffed with shrimp au gratin sauce, topped with cheese, then broiled until golden brown.

Nick's Dance Hall comes alive on the weekends. Live Cajun music fills the place and gets your toes to tapping. Before long, you'll find yourself out on that huge dance floor, shuffling out a two-step and shouting "Aiieeee!"

Located at 123 South Second Street.

OLD ABSINTHE HOUSE • NEW ORLEANS

Absinthe is a particularly potent liquor, made from the flowers and leaves of wormwood, a medicinal plant. Often called "le Fee Verte," the Green Fairy, because of its pale emerald green color, it originated as an elixir in the late nineteenth century. Its highly intoxicating properties, however, made it wildly popular during the early twentieth century, especially with the artists and writers, who found inspiration in its hallucinogenic deliriums. Because it was thought to be highly addictive, Absinthe was banned in the U.S. and many European countries in 1915.

The Old Absinthe House, built in 1806, was originally an importing firm, then was converted into a corner grocery, selling food, tobacco, and fine Spanish liquor. Still later, it became a coffee house, where in 1874, mixologist Cayetano Ferrer created an Absinthe-based drink he called the "Old Absinthe House Frappe." The drink was so popular that the coffee house was renamed in its honor.

At the beginning of Prohibition, the long copper-topped wooden bar was slated to be destroyed as a statement against all the drinking and carousing that went on in those sinful times. However, a group of sinners sneaked in one night and, under the cover of darkness, moved the bar to a warehouse on Bourbon Street for safekeeping until better days.

It's around that historic bar that bar goers gather for an evening of drinking and fun. And, it's not the only original feature. Antique chandeliers (accompanied by more modern team football helmets and jersey) hang from exposed cypress beams. Authentic marble fountains with brass faucets, once used to drip water onto the sugar cubes that sweetened the absinthe, line the bar. You can still get an Old Absinthe House Frappe—now made with Herbsaint, a legal absinthe-like liquor.

And, don't forget to add your business card to the millions that adorn the walls. It's testimony to the bar's motto: Everyone you have known or ever will know eventually ends up at the Old Absinthe House.

Located at 240 Bourbon Street.

PAT O'BRIEN'S • NEW ORLEANS

Have Fun! That's the motto of this historic bar, which opened in 1933. It's a must-stop on your stumble through the Quarter. I mean, you simply cannot go home without a Pat O'Brien's Hurricane glass. It's a law or something.

The drink was invented right here in 1942, at a time when whiskey was in short supply but there was more than enough rum to go around. Back in those days, liquor salesmen required that

Pat O'Brien's is famous for its hurricanes.
Courtesy of New Orleans CVB.

bar owners buy as many as fifty cases of rum just to get one case of whiskey. To get rid of all that extra rum, Pat O'Brien came up with the fruity drink. And, no, it wasn't named for a

Eat, Drink, and Be Merry!

storm. The name came about because it was served in a glass that resembled a hurricane lamp.

You can stagger in just for the glass, or make it a night here, with dinner at the Courtyard Restaurant, followed by a night of carousing in the main bar and a visit to the burning fountain in the outdoor courtyard. For a more mellow time, there's the piano bar across the carriage way.

Located at 718 St. Peter Street.

THE PIG STAND • VILLE PLATTE

This little piggy went to Ville Platte, and, boy, are we glad he did. Right here in the heart of Cajun country, the Pig Stand serves up some of the best barbecue around. It's just a little hole in the wall, but experience tells us those are where to find the best food! If barbecue's not what you're hankering for, don't despair. There's plenty more on the menu. You'll find Southern favorites as well traditional Cajun fare. Best of all, most dishes run you about five bucks.

Located at 318 East Main Street.

PRESERVATION HALL • NEW ORLEANS

Music is the heartbeat of New Orleans. You don't walk through these historic streets. You strut to the syncopation of a jazz rhythm. Everywhere you go there's a melody wrapping itself around you. It fills your head and your heart with the tempo of a city that invites you to live and love and laugh.

If the music of New Orleans is in your soul, then Preservation Hall is where you'll want to spend your nights. It's dark and small, and they don't serve food or drinks. But they do serve up Hot Jazz, played in the traditional New Orleans style. It's jazz the way Jelly Roll Morton and Louis Armstrong played it, before modern jazz diluted it.

Located within an eighteenth century building, Preservation Hall was created in 1961 as a sanctuary to protect and honor New Orleans Jazz. It's become a premiere venue for musicians who revere the music and believe it should be kept alive.

Come early—for other jazz freaks have learned of it—and stake out a seat up front. The small charge covers the whole night, so stay as long as you like. Close your eyes while the music of a bygone era fills your head and, with just a little imagination, you can see ol' Satchemo himself up there, white handkerchief wiping away the sweat as he raises his

Preservation Hall was created to protect and honor New Orleans Jazz.
Courtesy of New Orleans CVB.

trumpet to lips. A dollar will get your request played, unless you wanna hear "The Saints Come Marching In." That one will cost you five bucks. But it's money well spent. You'll leave with the heart of New Orleans beating in your soul.

Located at 726 St. Peter Street.

Eat, Drink, and Be Merry!

SHADY BRADY'S • MANDEVILLE

Christopher Brady, owner and chef of Shady Brady's, serves up traditional Southern fare with a twist. It's fine dining, but with a menu that doesn't make you go "Huh?" Take for instance, the meatloaf. It's made with smoked veal, lightly seasoned with herbs, mopped, not with plain catsup, but with tomato garlic sauce, and encrusted from its time on the barbecue pit.

The fried green tomatoes are finished with a smooth shrimp remoulade, the fried oysters on the half shell swim in pools of blue cheese dressing, and the gumbo is thick with chunks of pulled pork charred from the barbecue pit. It's not your grandma's cooking, unless, of course, your grandma studied under Chef John Folse.

At Shady Brady's you can run the gamut, from succulent barbecue to tender filet mignon, all offered with traditional, sort of, sides, such as black-eyed peas (with a hint of cinnamon, perhaps?), smothered cabbage (is that roasted garlic?), mashed potatoes, and dessert-sweet corn pudding. Like we said, twisted Southern traditional.

Located at 301 Lafitte Street.

Better watch your step in our Strange But True Louisiana. You never know when the long arm of the law may reach out and nab you for breaking some of these strange but true laws!

1. It's against the law to steal even one crawfish.

2. You can walk down the street with an alcoholic drink in New Orleans. You can drink and drive. But don't fall over and block the sidewalk or you'll be arrested.

3. It's illegal to rob a bank, then shoot the teller with a water pistol.

4. It's illegal to throw food from a Mardi Gras float.

5. It's illegal to wear a goatee in public without a license.

6. Snoring is prohibited unless all the bedroom windows are closed and securely locked.

7. Couples shopping for beds are prohibited from trying it out by making love—or even simulating that activity.

8. It's against the law for taxi drivers to make love in the front seat of their taxis during a shift.

9. It's against the law for mourners at a wake to eat more than three sandwiches.

10. It's illegal to tie an alligator to a fire hydrant.

Funny Happenings Here

Inmates on bucking broncos. Outlaw shootouts. Mudbugs and music. There's funny goings on in Strange But True Louisiana.

ANGOLA PRISON RODEO • ANGOLA

The Bust Out is the beginning event of the forty-year-old Angola Prison Rodeo, where all competing inmates bust out of the chute astride their angry bulls at the same time. The last guy to hit the dirt wins. There's a lot of that going on—hitting the dirt—as cowboy inmates compete for the title of All-Around Cowboy in events such as Bull Dogging, where two inmates team to wrestle a bull to the ground, Bull Riding, and Bareback Bronco Riding.

In addition to these events, inmates compete in some even more wild and wooly events, where broken bones are a common hazard. There's Convict Poker, where inmates sit around a table playing poker. Sounds pretty tame, huh? Well, it's not. See, they're sitting in the middle of the ring with a ticked off bull on the loose. The last inmate to be knocked down by the bull wins. Then there's Wild Cow Milking, where teams of inmates chase wild cows around the arena, trying to get a little milk in their buckets. The first team to present a bucket with milk in it wins.

Funny Happenings Here

The rodeo concludes just as fast and furious as it begins. The ending event is called Guts and Glory. Yeah, the one spilling his guts in the dust, gets the glory. In this event, a wooden chip is tied to the horn of another ticked off bull that's set lose in the arena. The inmate who successfully removes the chip wins.

Begun back in 1965, the Angola Rodeo is the longest running prison rodeo in the country. And, no doubt, the most profitable. Last year, the rodeo brought in a cool million, with more than 7,500 folks attending. Profits, says Warden Burl Cain, go toward expansion of prison facilities, such as inmate recreation and the building of churches.

In addition to the rodeo, there are arts and crafts—done by inmates—and food concessions, which includes prison-made jambalaya. Cain says he sees the rodeo as a way to allow outsiders to see inmates as something more than animals and a way to rehabilitate inmates by raising their self-esteem.

That is, if they make it out in one piece. It's not called "The Wildest Show in the South" for nothing. Although, remarkably, despite the fact inmates have no opportunity to practice their bull and bronco riding during the year, there have been no deaths. There have been plenty of broken bones, however, and ambulance crews are always on hand.

So, what do the inmates get from it? Well, besides that self-esteem thing, if they win, the prize money is way more than the two cents an hour they earn in prison, money that can be sent home to help out their families. And they get a big break from the monotony of their day-to-day existence.

The Angola Prison Rodeo is held every Sunday afternoon in October and on one Sunday in April.

Bonnie and Clyde Festival • Gibsland

Of all the strange but true things we've told you about, this might be the strangest but truest. Gibsland is the only town in the country that celebrates the death of the country's most notorious criminal couples. Why, you say, would little Gibsland, Louisiana, be so interested in the deaths of Bonnie and Clyde? Because, we answer, Gibsland is where the two met their fates.

It happened on May 23, 1934, right out there on Ringold Road. Bonnie and Clyde had been on a two-year criminal tear, robbing banks and killing cops across four states. Despite their blood thirstiness, they had gained popularity with the Depression-era common folk, who saw them as modern-day Robin Hoods. And, indeed, they did have a good streak. For on that fateful day, out there on Ringold Road, they stopped to help a farmer change a flat, when they were ambushed by the coppers.

Suddenly machine-gunfire erupted from a copse of trees on the side of the road. Caught by surprise, Bonnie and Clyde had no chance to respond. Bullets zinged through the air and pierced blood and bone, forcing the couple into a last gruesome dance together. Then all was quiet. The two lay dead, their blood turning the dirt of Ringold Road to red. It was the most exciting thing that ever happened in Gibsland. So exciting, in fact, that the town reenacts the drama every year!

Funny Happenings Here

The Bonnie and Clyde Festival stages a reenactment of that gory scene, complete with the bullet-ridden car that appeared in the 1967 movie *Bonne and Clyde*. There are blazing guns, lots of fake blood, and reenactments of a bank robbery and a hostage situation.

Visitors get the opportunity to talk with relatives of Bonnie and Clyde, such as Clyde's nephew Buddy Barrow. Then there's Boots Hinton, whose father was one of the six lawmen who staged the ambush. In addition, there's a Friday evening presentation of historians, who discuss the minutia of Bonnie and Clyde's bloody two-year reign and their gory deaths. Of course, there're vendors selling all manner of stuff—from T-shirts to pieces of the pants Clyde was wearing at his death. Bring plenty of money for that, though. Each swatch costs $200.

Held annually on the weekend closest to May 23.

BUGGY FESTIVAL • CHURCH POINT

The road leading to Church Point was one of the last in the state to be paved. Because of that, buggies and wagons remained the town's main transportation into the early fifties, earning it the title Buggy Capital of the World.

That's why, when the town needed to raise funds to keep the local hospital open, they chose to host a Buggy Festival, a weekend of music, food, and fun. There's a whole slew of pageants, for beauties of all ages. The Buggy Festival Queen gets the honor of representing the town throughout the state.

The festival features plenty of good food; live music, the highlight of which is a children's accordion and fiddle contest;

dancing in the streets; a carnival, a buggy display; a baby crawling contest; a children's French speaking contest; and arts and crafts. The weekend culminates with a parade of buggies and wagons.

Held annually in June.

CONTRABAND DAYS • LAKE CHARLES

Contraband Days Festival is a twelve-day extravaganza celebrating the town's history with Louisiana's most famous pirate. Legend has it that Jean Lafitte and his band of pirates often hid out along the waterways of Lake Charles. In fact, says the legend, one of Lafitte's favorite hideouts was the bayou of Lake Charles. It's said that he hid a cache of gold and silver in this bayou, an act that gave Contraband Bayou its name.

The festivities kick off with the annual capturing of Lake Charles, with sword-wielding pirates and cannon-firing militia and a mayor who ends up in the drink. And the fun is just starting. There are twelve whole days of events, including a full carnival, helicopter rides, beach volleyball, a sailing regatta, a motorcycle rally, live music, fireworks, and plenty of good Cajun food. There are plenty of fun competitions, too, such as a Crawfish Eating Contest, Arm Wrestling, Men's Log Rolling, and a Kid's Costume Contest. Even your favorite canine can get into the act with a Doggie Log Boom Race. Get your doggie to run down that log, and you deserve Lafitte's lost treasure!

Drawing a crowd of two-hundred thousand pirate lovers, Contraband Days is one of the largest events in Southwest Louisiana. In its sixty-year history, it has gained much recognition and has won numerous awards.

Held annually the first two weeks in May.

Funny Happenings Here

FESTIVAL INTERNATIONAL DE LOUISIANE • LAFAYETTE

A premier cultural event, the Festival International de Louisiane has presented some of the most distinctive world musicians and performances in the country. The festival began in 1986 as a way to celebrate the French cultural heritage of southern Louisiana, which combines French, African, Caribbean, and Hispanic influences.

Every year, visual, performing, and culinary artists from Europe, Africa, Canada, and the Caribbean come to Louisiana to share their talents. Historic downtown Lafayette is transformed into an

The Festival International de Louisiane presents some of the most distinctive world musicians and performances in the country.
Courtesy of Louisiana Office of Tourism.

entertainment complex featuring six music stages, food courts, street musicians and artists, arts and crafts boutiques, art galleries, cultural workshops, international cooking demonstrations, and a world music store.

The country's largest free Francophone (French-speaking) event, the festival has presented performers from such diverse cultures as France, Haiti, Japan, Morocco, and Scandinavia.

Held annually in April.

FRENCH QUARTER FESTIVAL • NEW ORLEANS

The French Quarter Festival is the South's largest free music festival. Fifteen music stages set up throughout the Quarter showcase the best of New Orleans music. You'll find every music genre here— gospel, jazz, Latin, classical, and, of course, Cajun and Zydeco. You can boogie from stage to stage, sampling music, food, and drink as you go. And don't miss the World's Largest Jazz Brunch, catered by some of New Orleans's world-famous restaurants.

The French Quarter Festival features fifteen music stages.
Courtesy of Louisiana Office of Tourism.

Held annually in April.

FROG FESTIVAL • RAYNE

There's a hoppin' good time going on in Rayne. The town is internationally known as the Frog Capital of the World. See, back in the 1880s, Jacque, Edmond, and Gautran, the Weil Brothers, noticed that Rayne had a really large number of juicy, fat-legged "ouaouarons" (that's Quebec-talk for bull frogs).

Funny Happenings Here

They began exporting Rayne's bull frogs to restaurants in France. Pretty soon, Rayne was a hopping place.

Bull frogs are no longer exported from Rayne, but the town still celebrates the jumpy little amphibian with an annual festival. Rayne's Frog Festival kicks off with the World Championship Frog Jumping Contest and a fais-do-do, led by M'sieur Jacques, Rayne's froggy ambassador. After that, there's all sorts of frog-related events, such as the Lion's Club Frog Derby, where little girls dress their frogs up in cute costumes, then pit them against each other in a jumping contest. There's a pageant, where a local beauty is crowned the Frog Festival Queen; a Frog Festival Parade; children's activities; frog races; lots of good music; and plenty of good food. And, yes, frog is on the menu. In fact, the premier event of the festival is the frog eating competition, where contestants dressed in formal attire see who can eat the most frog legs.

Held annually in September.

Giant Omelette Celebration • Abbeville

There's an interesting story behind this festival. See, according to legend, when Napoleon and his army were traveling through the south of France, they stopped for the night in the small town of Bessieres. The next morning, the innkeeper made the emperor an omelette so tasty that Napoleon ordered the townspeople to gather up all the eggs in the village and prepare an omelette for his army. Reportedly, this was the beginning of the tradition of feeding omelettes to the poor at Easter. It's also how the omelette became the symbol of a worldwide fraternity known as the Confrerie.

In 1984, Abbeville decided they wanted to join this eggy Confrerie. So, three members of the Chamber of Commerce scrambled over to the town of Bessieres to attend the Easter Omelette Festival. Knighted as the first of Abbevilles Chevaliers, the three returned home determined to bring Abbeville closer to its French heritage. They'd join the sisterhood of six international cities who celebrate the omelette with an omelette festival.

Abbeville's Giant Omelette Festival is truly an international event, with foreign representatives from each of the six sister cities attending. They join in the festivities and

Local chefs prepare for the Giant Omelette Celebration.
Courtesy of Giant Omelette Celebration.

experience Louisiana's rich heritage and joie de vivre. Festival events include forty juried artists displaying their works in Abbeville's town square, live music and entertainment, kid's activities, an antique car show, and a tour of local homes.

Now, if you kinda figured there'd be a few eggs broken in a Giant Omelette Celebration, you'd be right. Five thousand of them, to be exact. On Sunday, the visiting dignitaries gather with local chefs for the cooking of the Giant Omelette. It's the biggest darn omelette you'll ever see! And, it's free. So, don't eat before you come!

Held annually in November.

Gumbo Festival • Bridge City

Bridge City is the Gumbo Capital of the World. We know it's so because in 1934, Louisiana's governor issued a proclamation declaring it. Well, of course, an honor such as that must be celebrated with a festival!

There are plenty of fun activities during this festival—live music, a fais-do-do, the crowning of a Miss Creole Gumbo and King Creole Gumbo, and carnival rides. But the main attraction here is the food. More than two thousand gallons of gumbo are served, along with jambalaya, New Orleans-style red beans and rice, hamburgers, homemade cakes and candies, and funnel cakes. In addition, there's a gumbo cooking contest that's open to all comers. So, get your granny's favorite recipe and come on down.

Held annually in October.

Jambalaya Festival • Gonzales

You knew there had to be a "Jambalaya Capital of the World." We don't know if there was a proclamation, but the town of Gonzales lays claim to the title. And, guess what? They have a festival to celebrate it.

And guess what they do? Right! They cook jambalaya. In fact, they hold the World Jambalaya Cooking Championship and the Champ of Champions Cooking Contest, where past champions vie for the "best of the best" title. There's also the Mini-Pot Jambalaya Contest, a festival tradition since 1972. In this contest, competitors cook jambalaya in a tiny pot. In all the cooking contests, the jambalaya is cooked over a wood fire.

In addition, there's carnival rides, a car show, live music, and dancing in the streets.

Held annually in May.

LOUISIANA SHRIMP AND PETROLEUM FESTIVAL • MORGAN CITY

Doesn't sound too appetizing, but it all makes perfect sense. You see, this festival started out in 1936 as the Louisiana Shrimp Festival. It came about when Morgan City got its first boatload of jumbo shrimp from the deepest waters ever fished by a small boat. On that Labor Day, the workers of Morgan City—shrimpers, alligator and frog hunters, crabbers, dock workers, and oyster

The Louisiana Shrimp and Petroleum Festival was voted Best Festival by the Louisiana Association of Fairs and Festivals.
Courtesy of Louisiana Office of Tourism.

men—staged a friendly labor demonstration, taking to the streets for an impromptu parade. This was the first festival.

Funny Happenings Here

Well, time marched on, times changed, and Morgan City changed with them. The ocean still provided the city with much of its bounty, but by 1967, there was a new business in town. And petroleum was its name. So, the festival's name was changed. But the idea was the same, to honor the workers of Morgan City and celebrate the bounties the town has enjoyed.

The Louisiana Shrimp and Petroleum Festival is the oldest state-chartered harvest festival in Louisiana. A five-day gala, jam-packed with all the usual festival festivities—lots of good food, plenty of live music, arts and crafts, a huge parade, beauty pageants, fun and funny contests, and other activities. But the Louisiana Shrimp and Petroleum Festival has something most festivals don't. And it all happens on Sunday.

On Sunday, the traditions of the two disparate industries are celebrated with the historic Blessing of the Fleet and a water parade, featuring brightly decorated shrimp boats, pleasure crafts, and oil industry muscle boats. The pageantry culminates with the annual champagne toast between the king and queen. Doesn't sound all that exciting? Well, consider that the king and queen are on different vessels and that each vessel is made of tons of steel. The ships are brought together in a breathtaking bow-kiss, while the king and queen clink their glasses.

The Louisiana Shrimp and Petroleum Festival brings tens of thousands of visitors to Morgan City. It was voted Best Festival by the Louisiana Association of Fairs and Festivals, and was selected as a Top 20 Event by the Southeast Tourism Society and a Top 100 Event by the American Bus Association. Even better, *Time* magazine said the festival was "one of the most unusual, the most down-home, the most moving, and the most fun the country has to offer."

Held annually the week of Labor Day.

MARDI GRAS • IT'S EVERYWHERE!

Mardi Gras in New Orleans is one of the largest celebrations in the country. With origins in ancient Rome, the festival was brought to America by French explorer Sieur d'Iberville in 1699. Celebrations were banned when New Orleans was under Spanish control, but resumed in 1827.

The first documented parade occurred in 1837, but violence surrounding the celebration brought a call to discontinue it. Mardi Gras was saved by six New Orleans, who formed the Comus organization.

Mardi Gras is one of the largest celebrations in the country.
Courtesy of New Orleans CVB.

The first group to use "krewe" as a description, they showed that Mardi Gras could be a safe and fun event. They also instituted the traditions of the secret Carnival society, of a parade with theme floats, and of the festive Mardi Gras Ball following the parade.

More traditions evolved as the years passed and the celebration grew. The King Cake tradition was introduced in 1871. The tradition originated in Europe in the twelfth century during a celebration honoring the coming of the three wise men bearing gifts for the Christ Child twelve days after Christmas. It was called the Feast of the Epiphany, Twelfth Night, or King's Day. A main part of the celebration was the baking of the King's Cake, which honored the three kings. The cakes were circular to signify the circular route the kings took to confuse King Herod, who wanted to kill the Christ Child. A bean, pea, or coin was baked inside the cake, and the person who found it was declared King for the day and was believed to have good luck all year.

The Twelfth Night Revelers began the tradition in New Orleans by presenting a cake with a golden bean inside to a young New Orleans woman. This young woman was the first Mardi Gras Queen.

In 1872, the Krewe of Rex made its debut and began the King of Carnival tradition. This krewe also instituted the official colors of Mardi Gras. According to legend, Grand Duke Alexis Romanoff of Russia was visiting New Orleans and the Krewe of Rex asked him to choose the colors. He chose the colors of the House of Ramanoff—purple (symbolizing justice), green (symbolizing faith), and gold (symbolizing power).

Mardi Gras was suspended during the Civil War and in 1918 and 1919, the bloody years of World War I. It struggled, but survived both Prohibition and the Great Depression.

It can be a wild, bawdy time for people to forget their troubles and inhibitions. At least in certain places. But not everywhere. Stay out of the French Quarter, and you'll find a fun celebration where the kid's eyes won't be bugging out and the embarrassing questions will be kept to a minimum. The oak-lined St. Charles Avenue is a good place to enjoy the colorful floats and marching bands without the drunken revelry. There are family picnics and barbecues along the parade route.

Mardi Gras is celebrated throughout Louisiana. These celebrations are much less rowdy than in New Orleans. The following are some of the more significant celebrations.

New Roads hosts the oldest Mardi Gras celebration outside of New Orleans. Held on Shrove Tuesday, the celebration features up to thirty floats—built new each year—marching bands, and tons of beads, toys, and trinkets to be thrown.

Lafayette's celebration attracts around two hundred fifty thousand people annually. A family-friendly celebration, it's been an annual event since 1934, with many Hollywood celebrities serving as Grand Marshals.

Metairie, Houma, La Place, Chalmette, and Thibodaux all have large, family-friendly celebrations with multiple parades.

Some towns are noted for their Courir du Mardi Gras, the "Running of the Mardi Gras." In this tradition, which has its roots in Medieval times, revelers on horseback ride through the countryside begging for ingredients to a large communal meal—usually gumbo—that will be made later that day. Led by "Le Capitaine," the costumed riders go from house to house, where the homeowner may comply with the request, usually turning over vegetables or live animals, such as a chicken or a pig. The homeowner may turn the animal loose, making the runners have to chase it. The homeowner may also refuse to give anything, in which case, Le Capitaine may order his runners to steal it. A good time is had by all. Some of the towns staging Courir du Mardi Gras include Mamou, Iota, Church Point, Eunice, Ville Platte, and Elton.

MUDBUG MADNESS • SHREVEPORT

Because their town is located near the Louisiana-Texas line, the folks of Shreveport are accustomed to hearing disparaging comments from their fellow citizens. A couple of the most repeated include, "You people in Shreveport are more like Texans than anything else. You're hardly part of Louisiana at all."

Now the good folks of Shreveport take exception to these words. They're Louisianans right down to their souls. So, in 1984, they decided to put shut to those comments and pay homage to one of Louisiana's most cherished traditions, the crawfish boil. But this wasn't going to be just a crawfish boil, it was goin' to be the granddaddy of all crawfish boils. It would be Mudbug Madness!

And that's just what it is. What started as a two-day festival has morphed into a four-day extravaganza featuring renowned Cajun, zydeco, blues, and jazz—no Western music allowed—artists, wild and crazy contests, and some of the best Cajun Cuisine around. It's become so famous that it's recognized as one of the Southeast Tourism Society's Top 20 Events.

Held annually on Memorial Day Weekend.

OIL AND GAS FESTIVAL • EVANGELINE

From crawfish to oil. Not such a leap, since both are Louisiana staples. Evangeline is the birthplace of the Louisiana oil industry. Oil was discovered here more than one hundred years ago. Many of the town's citizens worked the early oil rigs and many today are fourth generation oil workers.

Every year, the town honors the industry with a good ol' fashioned Cajun shindig. With live music playing all day long, there's plenty of Cajun food, kid's games, a live auction, Bingo, and a joke-telling contest. The highlight of the weekend has to be the Oil and Gas Beauty Pageant and the crowning of Miss Evangeline Oil and Gas Festival.

Held annually in September.

VOODOO MUSIC EXPERIENCE • NEW ORLEANS

Music is New Orleans. New Orleans is music. New Orleans is also revelry in weird costumes. And all of that comes together in the Voodoo Music Experience, a two-day festival showcasing the wide variety of New Orleans music.

If you were anywhere but New Orleans, you might find it just a tad weird to see headlining musicians in pink feather headdresses, but here the Halloween theme (the festival is held the last weekend in October) never turns a head. They're too busy groovin' to the music.

The Voodoo Music Experience features up to sixty bands on six stages. It's one of the state's largest festivals, drawing in nearly 100,000 music fanatics. Held in the City Park, a few miles from the French Quarter, the festival is two days of nonstop music. One of the most popular venues is the Preservation Hall tent, where national and local jazz musicians have folks dancing on the tables. There are, of course, plenty of food and drinks. With Southern Comfort as a main sponsor, you're assured that alcoholic beverages are allowed.

Held annually the last weekend in October.

ZYDECO MUSIC FESTIVAL • OPELOUSAS

Back in the olden days, the folks in the Creole Community would come together during harvest time and work together to get the job done. Similarly, when it was time to slaughter a few hogs, a family would hold a bouchere (hog butchering) and everyone in the community would lend a hand.

When the work was done, there would be a La La (French Creole for house dance), with music and food and dancing. La Las also were held if a family was experiencing a cash crunch. The family would clear the living room of furniture and charge a ten or fifteen cent fee. They would sell gumbo and homemade beer and the whole town would turn out for more music and dancing.

The instruments used to play La La music were the fiddle, triangles, and the accordion, accompanied by some household devices—the scrub board (the frottoir) and spoons. La La music was a blending of the Cajun and Black Creole cultures. It was christened Zydeco by the King of Zydeco Clifton Chenier, who recorded the song "Les Haricorts Sont Pas Saler (The String Beans Are Not Salty). The word "Zydeco" is a French Creole variation for haricorts. Chenier started calling his music Zydeco—perhaps because it was so snappy.

However it got its name, Zydeco music is a pure product of southern Louisiana.

In 1981, a group of southwestern Louisiana folks, concerned that Zydeco was being lost, organized a festival to celebrate the music and keep it alive. It's now the world's largest Zydeco music festival. True to usual festival form, you'll find good Cajun/Creole food, arts and crafts booths, a King and Queen Ball, and activities for adults and kids.

Zydeco is dancin' music. First you start snapping your fingers. Then your foot starts tapping. And before you know it your whole body is filled with the music and you find yourself up on the dance floor, cutting a heck of a rug. It's so much fun you can't believe it's legal.

Held annually in September.